THE GREAT PYRAMID

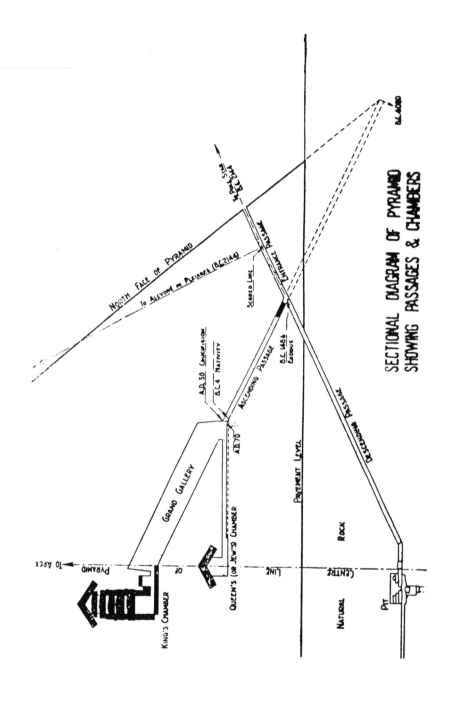

SECTIONAL DIAGRAM OF PYRAMID
SHOWING PASSAGES & CHAMBERS

"The Bible in Stone"

The Great Pyramid

Its Construction, Symbolism
and Chronology

By
BASIL STEWART

Author of
" Witness of the Great Pyramid "
" Mystery of the Great Pyramid "
" Times of the Gentiles "
" Bible Chronology "
and many others

Illustrated by Diagrams

FOURTH EDITION (Revised and Enlarged)

(Eighteenth Thousand)

SUN BOOKS
Sun Publishing Company

First Sun Books Printing...1992

Copyright © 1992 By Sun Publishing Company

First published: October 1925
Second Edition: May 1927
Third Edition: May 1931
Fourth Edition: April 1933

Sun Books
are Published by
Sun Publishing Company
P.O. Box 5588 Santa Fe,
NM 87502-5588 U.S.A.

ISBN: 0-89540-222-X

CONTENTS

DIAGRAMS

AN ANSWER TO SCOFFERS

*"The evidence of the truth of all Revelation
is so constructed as to be quite sufficient
for the humble and sincere who are ready to
believe ; while it is such as may be cavilled
at by any who wish to disbelieve."* (*Anon.*)

AUTHOR'S NOTE TO FOURTH EDITION

OPPORTUNITY has been taken, by the request for another issue of this introductory book on the Great Pyramid—a fact which indicates the increasing interest being taken in the subject—to revise it in accordance with the queries thereon that have since reached us, and to explain in somewhat greater detail features which appear to require further elucidation. A short chapter has been added on the builder of the pyramid, as ideas, not in accordance with the available evidence thereon, appear rather prevalent. A full discussion of the question, and the various traditions thereon, will be found in our two larger books on the Pyramid.

The intelligent enquirer will find herein all the various features of the Great Pyramid presented in concise yet comprehensive form, sufficient to enable him to understand clearly the true purpose for which this remarkable monument was erected by a now long-past civilization, and the manner in which the message it had to transmit has been conveyed, and why it is of such importance to us to-day. Technicalities have been avoided as much as possible, or when introduced at all have been expressed as simply as the scientific nature of the subject will allow.

[Matter enclosed in square brackets inserted in quotations from other authors is the present writer's.]

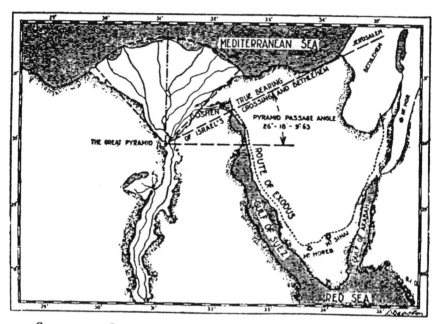

GEOGRAPHICAL POSITION OF THE GREAT PYRAMID, AND ALSO ITS RELATION
TO BETHLEHEM AND ISRAEL'S CROSSING OF THE RED SEA

*"In that day shall there be an altar to the Lord in the midst
of the land of Egypt, and a pillar at the border thereof to the
Lord. And it shall be for a sign and a witness unto the Lord of
hosts in the Land of Egypt."* (Isaiah xix, 19-20.)

THE GREAT PYRAMID

CHAPTER I

THE PROBLEM OF THE GREAT PYRAMID

EVEN as the group of pyramids standing on the plateau of Gizeh, a few miles south of Cairo, are far in advance of all other pyramids throughout Egypt, on the score of age, purity of form, excellence of construction and preservation, so is there one amongst this group which surpasses all the others—the Great Pyramid of Khufu (or Cheops—Greek form of name).

There is, indeed, no known period within historic times when the Great Pyramid was not famous, not only by virtue of its size and greater antiquity, but because of its unique construction. The result is its purpose has been a mattei of speculation from the earliest days, and has proved a most fertile source of enquiry from the time of Herodotus —regarded as the father of historians—down to the present. More, indeed, has been written about the Great Pyramid than about any other monument of antiquity.

Many traditional accounts, largely from Arab and Coptic sources, have come down to us, all, however, bearing a close resemblance to one another, showing them to be variants of the same originals with details added by their respective authors. All agree, however, in describing the Great Pyramid as an object of curiosity and mystery, combined with great antiquity, and such it has remained ever since it was built till quite recent times.

That a proper knowledge of its true purpose is only

1

becoming general to-day is because it was so constructed that only the science of the twentieth century would be able to interpret it. For over 3,000 years of the Pyramid's existence, till the time of the forced entry made in the 9th century of our era, no one had ever—as far as historically known—penetrated into its upper passages and chambers. All access thereto was pievented by the granite plug at the lower end of the First Ascending Passage, which was *built into position during construction.**

It is important to bear this fact in mind, since it is a clear constructional proof (amongst other proofs) against the tombic theory of the Great Pyramid advanced by Egyptologists. This theory is discussed in detail in the author's *Witness of the Great Pyramid* (2nd Ed.), pp. 14-28, and in his *Mystery of the Great Pyramid*, pp. 37-50, to which the reader is referred, and is shown to be erroneous from whatever point of view the theory be approached. It is an idea wholly borrowed from later pyramids ignorantly copied from the Great Pyramid, many of which were used for royal burial, but with which the Great Pyramid has nothing in common except in its outward form.

Egyptologists have applied the tombic theory to the Great Pyramid simply because they cannot conceive any other purpose for it, overlooking facts which disprove it because such did not appeal to them. Failure to appreciate this evidence is due to the fact that the Great Pyramid —unlike all other pyramids in Egypt—is a monumental piece of *engineering construction*, planned and erected on engineering principles, which consequently can only be appreciated and understood by the civil engineer con-

* Proofs of this will be found in our larger books on this subject. The usual idea is that it was stored in the Grand Gallery above until required, and then afterwards allowed to slide down the Passage to block its lower end. More than one engineering reason can be given to show this is impossible, but apart from this, the passage immediately *above* the plug is one-tenth of an inch—both in width and depth—*less* than the plug itself.

versant with constructional work on a large scale. *It is, therefore, not a problem for the Egyptologist to solve.*

It is for this reason that the many capable engineers who have studied the Great Pyramid, supplemented by architects, mathematicians and astronomers—of whom the most recent is the distinguished French astronomer, the Abbé Moreux (*vide* his *Mysterious Science of the Pharaohs*)—have, practically without exception, disagreed with the Egyptological theory of the Great Pyramid.

"One should never ask a savant the secrets of the universe that are not in his particular showcase : he takes no interest in them." The truth of this shrewd—if cynical—observation on the part of the late Anatole France concerning scientists, is nowhere better illustrated than in the attitude of Egyptologists towards the problem of the Great Pyramid. Evidence disproving their theory of it as a tomb finds no place in their "showcase." The most that can be said for the tombic theory of the Great Pyramid is that it is just a possible, but very improbable, supposition.

The problem of the Great Pyramid, in fact, is, like its construction, unique. Though erected *in* Egypt, it is *not of Egyptian origin*, and it is because Egyptologists, as a body, have failed to recognize this fact that they have been unable to discover its true purpose, but have supposed it to be a tomb like other pyramids, *a theory for which no evidence can be produced in support.*

Though the Great Pyramid was the first true pyramid of any—being only exceeded in age by perhaps three others of pyramidal form, attempts having been made to convert two of them into true pyramids after the design of the Great Pyramid—none of the succeeding pyramids contain similar interior passages and chambers, but all copy, in varying degree, the Second Pyramid, erected in the reign of Khafra, successor to Khufu, with its single descending passage leading down to a supposed underground burial chamber, similar to the descending passage in the Great Pyramid.

This construction of a descending passage in the Great Pyramid, free of access, was a device on the part of the builder purposely to mislead—as was also his device in erecting a second pyramid alongside, almost as large as the first, with a similar passage—such imitators of pyramid-building as might arise after him. For the same reason he purposely made impossible of access the upper chambers and passages of the Great Pyramid, so that once the King's Chamber was roofed in, they were entirely sealed up, and therefore impossible of being copied in any later structure. For had this geometrical chart in stone—for such is its true purpose—been available for copying, it would have become lost amongst its three dozen or so spurious copies and the true one overlooked.* History has proved how successful the builder has been. Pyramid-building in Egypt ceased centuries before the upper passages of the Great Pyramid were first discovered in A.D. 820, and no other pyramid contains similar passages or chambers.

That the Great Pyramid was built for some very special purpose is clearly proved by its unique internal construction. There is no earlier structure—pyramid or otherwise—remotely resembling it, nor any later one ; neither is there any structure, nor series of structures, which indicate evolutionary steps leading up to this form of building. Before the Great Pyramid came into existence its peculiar system of passages and chambers was unknown ; after it no attempt has been made to reproduce them. There is simply a reversion to the type of sloping passage and underground tomb found in Zoser's Step Pyramid at Sakkara and Seneferu's "False" Pyramid of Meidoum, which, together with the latter's Great Pyramid at Dahshur, are the only structures of pyramidal *form* older than the

---

* There are about thirty-eight pyramids, or remains of pyramids, existing in Egypt to-day, some hardly recognisable as such.

Great Pyramid. These considerations by themselves, apart from the evidence contained in the Great Pyramid itself, should cause the logical mind one expects to find associated with the scientist to doubt gravely the tombic theory advanced for it by Egyptologists and others.

Even these earlier pyramids afford little evidence of the tombic theory of the Great Pyramid, but rather the reverse, since none of them was used as an actual tomb. Zoser's tomb exists at Bet Khallaf, while Seneferu's two pyramids are described as his *Kha*, or "spirit" pyramids, that is, cenotaphs ; and in any case, one would have sufficed for burial.

Further, the theory is neither upheld by tradition— except too vaguely to be at all trustworthy—nor by history, for both Herodotus and Diodorus Siculus distinctly state neither Khufu nor Khafra were buried in their respective pyramids.

The fact that neither the Great Pyramid nor the few earlier structures of this form were used as tombs, but that later pyramids were, shows the Egyptians of that day did not themselves know the purpose the architect had in erecting the Great Pyramid, but, like opinion ever since, down to present day Egyptologists, regarded it as a mausoleum built to perpetuate his name. Hence attempts made by subsequent monarchs to copy it, and their adoption of this form of burial place.

These earlier structures clearly indicate a period of experimental building in order to train the Egyptian workmen towards attaining the manual skill necessary in erecting the Great Pyramid. It is significant in this respect to note that, while the earliest tombs were constructed in brick and later in stone, the reverse is the case with the pyramids.

Thus, the Step Pyramid at Sakkara, built in the reign of Zoser (2707—2688 B.C.), a monarch of the Third Dynasty, is constructed in limestone, and was originally an oblong *mastaba*, or tomb with sloping sides, afterwards converted into the form of a pyramid by the addition of successive layers of masonry enclosing the original structure. It was thus built on the accretion plan, the defects of which are shown by the dilapidated condition in which it—and the Pyramid of Meidoum, also built on this principle—now stands.

The next pyramid—that of Seneferu (2669—2645 B.C.), the last king of the Third Dynasty, at Meidoum, the most southerly of the Egyptian pyramids—reveals larger and better worked blocks, and with much finer joints than Zoser's, indicating greater skill on the part of the workmen, but still shows the defective system of accretion building and its resultant failure. It also was built over a *mastaba*.

Following this came Seneferu's Great Stone Pyramid of Dahshur (built at the same time as his Meidoum pyramid), also known as the North Stone Pyramid of Dahshur, the first pyramid in which its masonry is correctly bonded and free from continuous straight joints. It thus nearly approaches the superlative workmanship of the Great Pyramid, and stands on about an equal footing in this respect with the Second Pyramid of Gizeh, with which it is also almost identical in size. Strictly speaking, therefore, Seneferu's Dahshur pyramid is the earliest true stone-constructed pyramid in existence. Its *design*, however, is due to the Great Pyramid, since the plans of the latter were in existence before its construction commenced. It is, therefore, perfectly correct to claim that the Great Pyramid was the first true pyramid of any. That the plans of the Great Pyramid were in existence at the time of Seneferu is borne out, not only by the true pyramidal form of his Dahshur pyramid, but by the statement of Petrie that "Seneferu's pyramid of Dahshur had chambers roofed like the gallery in the Great Pyramid by successive over-lappings of stone, the roof rising to a great height, with no less than eleven projections on each side" (*Pyramids and Temples of Gizeh*), a unique form of construction not found elsewhere.

There is also a second stone pyramid at Dahshur (besides three much smaller—and later—ones of brick) known as its Southern Stone Pyramid, sometimes referred to as the Blunt Pyramid from the fact that its upper part has been finished off at a flatter angle, as if the builders had found the task of completion too great and had altered the slope in order to reach the apex sooner.

The writer has been unable to find any reference to the possible builder of this Blunt Pyramid of Dahshur, but as it is nearly the same size as its companion, and therefore nearly the size of the Second Pyramid of Gizeh, it is probably more or less contemporary with it. This seems to be inferred also from Petrie's reference to it in conjunction with Seneferu's Dahshur pyramid, which we have shown belonged to an era of experimental building (only, however, as regards certain structural details, *not* as regards the internal arrangement of passages and chambers) previous to the construction of the Great Pyramid. Petrie confirms this by remarking of *both* these Dahshur pyramids that "the builders seem to be feeling their way, rather than falling off in copying existing models."

Thus, not only does pyramid construction previous to that of the Great Pyramid show a steady improvement in form, but also in method and craftsmanship, both reaching perfection in the Great Pyramid, after which deterioration set in, and the high standard then attained failed to be maintained. After the construction of the Second Pyramid, commenced immediately after the Great Pyramid and while the skill which erected it was still available, successive pyramids not only diminish rapidly in size, but also in quality of construction. And this perfection of workmanship was reached in practically fifty years only, the Great Pyramid having been constructed little more than half a century after the first pyramid was begun. The latest pyramids of all—those of the Twelfth Dynasty—deteriorated into structures of mud-bricks faced with stone, many of which have crumbled away into nothing.

The true era of pyramid building extended from the Third to the Sixth Dynasties inclusive, constituting the stone pyramid age. Then followed a long period of quiescence due to foreign invasions and occupation, after which pyramid construction was resumed again under the Twelfth Dynasty (*c.* 2000 to 1850 B.C.), the end of which saw the close of pyramid building in Egypt.

The conclusions reached concerning the problem of the Great Pyramid show that it was erected by members of a former civilization, Asiatic or Arabian in origin (refer Ch. II, *Mystery of the Great Pyramid*), which entered Egypt and organized the building of the Great Pyramid ; that this civilization possessed knowledge and faculties far in advance of all contemporary civilizations, but which became largely lost to the human race, only to be regained to any great extent in modern times ; that the Pyramid was built under Divine inspiration with the purpose of transmitting a message and warning to a civilization then unborn, which would be able to decipher that message and understand its warning ; that the wonderful scientific features embodied in its exterior construction were intended to draw attention to its interior wherein this message was hid ; and finally, that this message is addressed to the present age and particularly to the British race.

Regarding the scientific elements incorporated in the Pyramid's construction, such as are found in no other pyramid in Egypt, it does not necessarily follow it was erected to enshrine this knowledge, however such may have been attained. This scientific knowledge was merely made the channel whereby was conveyed to a future civilization, able to comprehend it, the particular message the architect was inspired to give. This is proved by the fact that it is presented in the language and terms of *modern exact science ;* hence the inability of all previous generations to understand the Great Pyramid or its purpose. And the message therein revealed is the same as the message of the Bible : to proclaim Christ as the Saviour and Deliverer of mankind, at the same time warning us of the time and circumstances of His Coming, to the end that, if we heeded it, we might be prepared for that great event.

This message is given in the form of a huge graph or geometrical diagram, represented by the pyramid's passages and chambers, the structural changes therein defining the dates of epoch-making events in world-history. Sceptics will say, of course, that such an idea is so improbable as to be dismissed at once from further consideration. It is, however, surely just as reasonable for one person to leave a record of future history in the form of a chart, expressed geometrically in the lines of a building—a form of representation precisely analogous to the graphical methods (known as "graphic statics") employed in the solution of problems by the civil engineer—as it is for others to commit a similar record to writing, as has been done in the Bible, all acting under Divine inspiration. For it is important to remember that the belief that the Great Pyramid *does* owe its origin to Divine inspiration, and *does* reveal a Divine revelation, is not an idea of this twentieth century.* On the contrary, it is as old as the Pyramid itself, and permeates the literary traditions of ancient Egypt, while the same revelation, which became distorted and lost in its true application, existed all over the ancient East from the earliest times.

It is hardly surprising, therefore, that we find the Great Pyramid referred to in Scripture, and its true purpose

---

* Mr. Lewis Spence, in the Preface to his *Mysteries of Egypt* (Rider), truly remarks : "For that school of archæology which, uninspired itself, denies and abhors inspiration, I can only profess that serene amusement with which archæologists of the future will assuredly regard it."

B

therein revealed as "a sign and a witness unto the Lord in the land of Egypt" (Isaiah xix, 19-20), towards the close of the "latter days"—the era of the "consummation" of Dan. ix, 27 (1891-1936—refer chart in our *Times of the Gentiles,* No. 13)—the very period for which its message was given, and in the scientific terms of which it is purposely expressed.

That the Great Pyramid is the structure referred to by Isaiah is shown by the fact that it *alone* fulfils *all* the conditions therein set out*—the *nature* of this "witness"; the *geographical position* thereof (see diagram p. viii), and the *time* of its discovery. Its geographical position is in itself sufficient to establish the identity of Isaiah's reference. Situated at the centre of the arc embracing the curved shore-line of Egypt, it is literally "in the midst (or centre) of the land of Egypt," which prophetically and historically is that part of it forming the Delta. Its meridian also divides the Delta into two equal parts, and being at the same time on the edge of the Libyan desert it is also "at the border" of Egypt, at its extreme southern limit, and the natural dividing line between Upper and Lower Egypt.

Sceptics have argued that since neither Isaiah nor any other writer in Scripture (e.g. Jeremiah, who also refers to it indirectly—xxxii, 20) refer to any pyramid as such, the foregoing application is far-fetched.

Since, however, the word "pyramid" did not come into use till long after the time of Isaiah, who had no equivalent in Hebrew for it, he could only describe it as a "monument," which is the correct meaning of the word *matsebhah,* translated "pillar" in the A.V.—"a pillar at the border thereof" (of Egypt).

On this point there is the following interesting comment by the late Moses Margoliouth, when editor of the *Hebrew*

---

* Neither the temple and altar erected by Onias at Leontopolis, 173 B.C., nor the Jewish temple at Yeb (referred to by Jeremiah) sixth century B.C., to both of which Isaiah's words have been applied, fulfil all these conditions, and only the first condition (an altar) improperly ; the other two not at all.

Christian Witness (vol. for 1875, pp. 541-2).* "We are pretty sure that if the translators of the A.V. of the Bible had been acquainted with these structures (the pyramids), and their mode of erection, which the Egyptians called *piromi*, the Greeks *pyramidos*, and Shakespeare, after the Greeks, *pyramid* [See Sonnet 123], they—the translators— would have employed the last-named term (pyramid) in the above Scripture passage. . . . We consider Professor Smyth justified in considering the word *matsebhah* in Isaiah xix to mean a pyramid."

The use by Isaiah of two words—an *altar* and a *pillar*— is intended to signify *two* characteristics embodied in *one* structure ; not two separate erections—a monument incorporating therein certain scientific and other truths, and at the same time an altar of *witness* (not of sacrifice— an important distinction, but one often overlooked) to the Almighty Who revealed these truths to the architect. In other words, a *memorial altar*.

While surprise may be expressed that anyone should build such a gigantic structure as the Great Pyramid merely for the purpose of prophetic chronology—a purpose, too, which would not be revealed till many centuries later—this form of representation was employed because, while written records are liable to perish and, when they survive, to be misread, a structure like the Great Pyramid is virtually indestructible and incapable of being distorted (as the written word of the Bible unfortunately has been), *provided the method of representation used is understood and properly applied.*

That various theories and interpretations have been read into the Great Pyramid's structure, is simply because their exponents have failed to understand the *language* employed by the builder—*geometry*—and the laws that govern it, or

* Quoted from Mrs. Bristowe's *The Man Who Built the Great Pyramid* (Williams & Norgate), p. 187.

to follow the indications supplied by him for its interpretation.

That the whole basis of the Great Pyramid is geometry, and that it was raised as an imperishable monument to the geometrical and mathematical science of a former civilization, is corroborated by Sir Flinders Petrie, who says: "The artistic motive was clearly a love of geometrical idea. The geometrical properties united by the form chosen are beyond a casual chance, and point to a great appreciation and study of geometry."

No more exact sciences exist than mathematics and geometry. Without them astronomy would be impossible. Any form of representation, therefore, based thereon, such as that embodied in the Great Pyramid, cannot be other than accurate.

That some such scientific record of historical chronology is necessary will be admitted when it is mentioned that, from the Bible alone, considerably over two hundred different chronologies have been derived, ranging from 3483 to 6984 B.C. in their basal date (Adam). In addition, there are the numerous theories current respecting the chronologies of ancient Babylon, Assyria, and Egypt.

It is precisely for these reasons that the Great Pyramid was erected, and has come down to us sufficiently intact to enable us to read it. It supplies the key, as it were, to all chronology, and particularly Bible chronology and prophecy, which is simply history pre-written. And if this key be applied it will be found to fit the lock accurately.*

* Refer the author's *True Bible Chronology* (Routledge), showing precise agreement between Bible chronology and that revealed in the Pyramid.

CHAPTER II

CONSTRUCTIONAL AND ASTRONOMICAL FEATURES OF THE GREAT PYRAMID

THE unit of measurement employed in the construction of the Great Pyramid is the Polar,* Primitive, or Pyramid inch, and the cubit of twenty-five such inches, identical with the Hebrew or sacred cubit. This is one proof that the Great Pyramid is not of Egyptian origin, since these units of measure were not native to Egypt, though the Egyptian measures were derived from them by an accurate but rule-of-thumb system of equivalents. These units, therefore, are the oldest standards of linear measure in existence, introduced by members of the Adamic civilization, who transmitted these standards to posterity in the construction of the Great Pyramid.

This brings us to the first point clearly indicating the particular significance of the Great Pyramid for the Anglo-Saxon race, for our inch varies from the Pyramid inch by only a thousandth part (1,000 Pyramid inches equals 1,001 British inches), while originally they were identical, this minute difference being due to lapse of time, and to the fact that for long periods we had no proper standards of length for comparison. And long before this evidence of the Great Pyramid connecting our linear measures with those of the Israelites—and earlier—came to light, Sir Isaac Newton drew a similar conclusion that the Hebrew cubit equalled twenty-five of our inches.

* *Polar* inch, because it is based upon the Earth's Polar diameter which measures 500 million such inches. It is therefore a truly scientific, earth-commensurable unit.

18

It has been stated, presumably to discredit this scientific theory of the Great Pyramid, that the Pyramid inch has been invented to suit the theory.

Since, however, the external features of the Great Pyramid form a geometrical representation of the earth and its orbit, the unit employed for such representation must necessarily be an earth-commensurable one, and the only scientifically correct dimension from which such a unit could be derived is the *straight* line of the earth's polar axis, not its irregularly curved surface from which the much-vaunted continental metre is (incorrectly) deduced. The earth's polar axis, too, is the one standard distance common to all countries throughout the world. If, therefore, all their standards of length were suddenly lost, they would be obliged to base their new ones upon the earth's polar diameter, and the unit adopted would have to be the polar (or Great Pyramid) inch. It is in this unit, too, that certain astronomical values of the orbit of the earth are found expressed with mathematical accuracy, *and in no other.*

Had it not been, therefore, for the preservation by the English-speaking peoples of their inherited measure—the inch—which has not only survived from the remotest antiquity, but has defeated the various attempts that have been made from time to time to displace it by the unscientific metre, the meaning of the Great Pyramid would never have been revealed, for otherwise the key to it would have been lost, and this witness in the land of Egypt would never have been unlocked. It is not surprising, therefore, that all who have been instrumental in deciphering it have belonged to the Anglo-Saxon race.

Corroboration of this identity between ourselves and the race who built the Great Pyramid is given by Professor Waddell in his *Phœnician Origin of Britons, Scots and Anglo-Saxons*, first published in 1924, working along entirely different lines of investigation. Waddell not only shows that the allegory of a Messiah or Saviour—an allegory revealed in the Great Pyramid—existed in all the literary systems of the ancient East (including Egypt in its so-called "Book of the Dead") even as far back as 3,000 B.C., or before the era of the Great Pyramid, but also that this universal prophecy likewise refers to a nation of "builders"—identical with the "building-race" of Great Pyramid prophecy—who are specified by the name of "Barats" or "Brits."

Further identification is given by the fact that the symbol of this nation was the year-circle, which is the basis of the mathematical system of the Great Pyramid itself, and was analogous to the solar-disc of Aten worship of the ancient Egyptians. This identification is itself corroborated by the fact that Stonehenge, the Eastern origin of which is established by archæology, folklore and tradition, is set out on precisely the same year-circle, proving that its builders were descended from the same race, and used the same system of metrology as the builders of the Great Pyramid. A circle of 3,652.42 pyramid inches circumference, equivalent to the number of days in a solar year on a scale of ten inches to a day, falls precisely internal to the outer ring of stones forming the circle of Stonehenge.* This fact proves that the astronomical conceptions of the ancient British megalithic builders originated in Egypt, where they reached their highest constructive expression in the erection of the Great Pyramid.

All measurements incorporated in the Great Pyramid belong to this mathematical system of the solar year expressed as a circle ; that is to say, they are mathematically related to, or derived from, a value of 36,524.2, 3,652.42, or 365.242 pyramid inches. It is owing to this fact that the intended measurements of any part of the Pyramid's passage system can be calculated to a degree of accuracy impossible by direct tape-measuring, which cannot

* A circle of this circumference measures 1,163 British inches in diameter.

do more than confirm the theoretical intention, which latter alone can give the precise dates defined in the Pyramid's chronograph.

A feature unique to the Great Pyramid in its external proportions is that its height is so proportioned to its base that it is analogous to the figure of a circle ; that is to say, the circumference of a circle described with a radius equal to the vertical height of the Pyramid (5,813 inches) will measure, as nearly as possible, the perimeter of the Pyramid's square base.

Because the Great Pyramid thus displays this peculiar proportion of height to base, it has been stated that its builder has solved the problem of "squaring the circle." This problem, however, is impossible of *exact* solution either arithmetically or by geometry : arithmetically, because the ratio of the circumference of a circle to its diameter (generally expressed as 3.14159 . . .) cannot be exactly expressed in figures, and has been calculated to over 200 places of decimals without reaching finality. Neither can it be solved geometrically, because there is no geometrical method of drawing a straight line equal in length to the circumference of a given circle, and by a "geometrical solution" is meant, of course, *a solution which involves no postulates outside those of Euclid.** What the Great Pyramid does achieve is to bring the problem as near a *practical* solution as can be done.

To assert, as practically all Pyramid investigators in the past have done, that the Great Pyramid "squares the circle," is to go beyond what its geometry reveals. Its proportions are such that its vertical height is to *twice* its base side as the diameter of a circle is to its circumference : or, expressed mathematically—5,813 : 18,262 : : 1 : 3.14159.

---

* In view of claims made from time to time purporting to have "squared the circle" (analogous in a way to the claims of perpetual motionalists), this condition is all-important.

In other words, the geometry of the Great Pyramid defines equality of *boundaries*, which is *not* the same as equality of *areas*. To say the Pyramid "squares the circle" is to assume boundaries and areas denote the same thing ; but the circle has this peculiar property—*that of all plane figures having the same perimeter, the circle contains the greatest area.* Hence a circle described with a radius equal to the vertical height of the Pyramid will contain a larger area than its square base.

A circle to give equal area would be 10,303.80 pyramid inches in diameter, against a diameter of 11,626.02 pyramid inches for a circle with radius equivalent to the Pyramid's height. Such an equal-area circle, on a scale of 1/100th, is defined in the Pyramid's Ante-chamber (see p. 83 *post*). Also the length of the *granite* floor in the Ante-chamber defines (on scale 1/100) the side of a square whose area equals area of circle with radius = height of Pyramid.

A conspicuous feature of the Great Pyramid, and one that has always evoked the highest praise, is the extraordinary accuracy of workmanship with which it has been built, an accuracy all the more remarkable when the size of the structure itself, and of the individual stones composing it, are taken into account. It is hardly an exaggeration to say that the largest, and almost the oldest, megalithic building in the world has been put together with the precision of a chronometer. Sir Flinders Petrie likens the accuracy of workmanship to that of modern optical work, and it is particularly noticeable in the outside casing stones (now demolished except for a few at the base), and in the Grand Gallery and King's Chamber internally.

While a primary object of the casing-stones—which were of limestone, since this material resists weathering better than the granite of which the inner core of the pyramid is constructed—was to protect this inner core, they also served another highly important function. For the Great

Pyramid embodied in its external surfaces the properties of a sundial on a gigantic scale, and it was designed to effect this purpose mainly by reflected sunlight ; hence the selection of the whitest limestone, and the extreme fineness of the joints to ensure perfect smoothness and uniformity of surface.

One of the principal objects of early pyramid-building in Egypt, as indicated by the first three pyramids on the Gizeh plateau, was to record the annual recurrence of the seasons throughout the year, astronomical and agricultural. Hence their great size, so as to be visible over a wide area, their accuracy of orientation* and workmanship, as these conditions were essential to fulfil the purpose of a huge sundial of the seasons.

"Experiments and investigations," writes Mr. Cotsworth in his *Rational Almanac* (1904), "have led me to believe that the real object of these stupendous erections—the pyramids of Egypt, Mexico and other countries— was to determine the seasons and exact length of the year by their regular graded and recurring shadows."

That such was the function of the Great Pyramid is indicated by the beautifully wrought pavement surrounding it, which should be distinguished from the platform on which the pyramid itself rests. This pavement forms just such a level "shadow floor" (refer Piazzi Smyth's *Our Inheritance*, plate vi), purposely extended on the north side by the builders to allow originally (it has since been partly destroyed) for the 268 feet required for the longest range of shadow.

It was this particular use of the Great Pyramid as a huge sundial—apart from its allegorical significance (fully ex-

* In this respect the Great Pyramid was—*and still is*—the most accurately oriented edifice in existence. Even to-day, after 4,500 years of earth "crust-creep," earthquake-shocks, and other causes, it is only *three minutes and six seconds* (an almost infinitesimal amount under all the circumstances) off true astronomical north, as ascertained by a recent Egyptian Government survey.

plained in our *Mystery of the Great Pyramid*)—which caused it to be named *Khut*, or "Light,"* from which comes the origin of the word "pyramid," or "light-measures," signifying its double purpose as a "beacon of reflections," and a "monument of measures," astronomical and terrestrial.

Turning now to the Pyramid's system of passages and chambers, these are not constructed in the central vertical plane passing through the apex of the building, but are set some twenty-four feet to one side of it—actually 286 inches *eastward* of the true north to south axis. This "displacement," as it is termed, is one of the reasons why the Arabs, when they attempted to break into the Great Pyramid early in the ninth century A.D., failed to find the entrance in the north face, since they attacked it in the centre, and also at a point considerably below where the concealed door was situated. They consequently forced an entrance at random, eventually breaking into the entrance passage close by the granite plug, more or less by accident, some distance inside the masonry.

This amount by which the passages are displaced from the central plane is termed the Great Pyramid's "displacement factor," and has an important bearing upon the interpretation of the science and geometry incorporated in the structure.

This displacement of the entrance passage *east* of the true centre has apparently led many writers on this subject, when noting the fact that this passage pointed in the direction of the pole star, to infer that this displacement indicated the amount by which the pole star of that time— some 4,000 years ago—was east of the celestial North Pole. Since, however, the whole passage—regarding it in the light of a telescopic tube—throughout its length, runs true north and south, its astronomical application would be just as valuable and accurate if it was exactly central with the

---

* The ancient Egyptians gave the name *Ur*, or "Great," to Khafra's Pyramid, generally referred to as the Second Pyramid of Gizeh.

vertical plane through the apex of the pyramid, for it is fairly obvious that its actual displacement 286 inches east of this plane, if produced to the pole star, whose distance is infinite in comparison, means nothing at all. In fact, the whole pyramid might be moved a hundred miles eastward or westward of its present site without making any apparent difference in the position of the star, since even a hundred miles is as nothing compared to the enormous distance separating us from the heavenly body.

From the entrance in the north face on the nineteenth masonry course, a passage, known as the Entrance Passage, about forty-seven inches high, descends steeply till nearly on a level with the outside pavement. At this point the Ascending Passage commences, the point of junction, however, having been originally concealed by the roof-stone of the Descending Passage, which latter thus appeared to be the pyramid's sole passage leading down to an underground pit. It was the quarrying of the Arabs, when making their forced entry, which accidentally dislodged this roof-stone, thereby revealing the granite plug immediately over it. By cutting a passage round this plug through the softer limestone surrounding it, they eventually got into the Ascending Passage and chambers beyond. They found, however, neither mummy nor fabled treasure they had hoped to discover.

The Descending Passage continues down, through the natural rock, for a distance of 253 feet from its junction with the Ascending Passage, when it becomes horizontal and of slightly smaller bore for about twenty-seven feet, finally ending in a subterranean pit a hundred feet below the base-level of the pyramid. Running still southwards is a very narrow passage leading out of the pit and coming to a dead end in the rock after a length of about 53 feet. This subterranean pit, the floor of which is very uneven, is by far the largest of the chambers in the Great Pyramid, and measures forty-six feet long east to west (all the chambers have their longest axis so placed) by twenty-seven feet wide, compared to the King's Chamber measurements of thirty-four feet by seventeen feet.

The Ascending Passage continues upwards for a distance of 129 feet, when a similar Horizontal Passage is reached, which leads under the Grand Gallery to the so-called Queen's Chamber. In this chamber is a recess or niche, about fifteen feet high, and tapering in the form of over-hanging steps, like the walls of the Grand Gallery, from sixty-two inches wide at the foot to twenty inches at the top.

Various conjectures have been made as to the purpose of this niche, one being that a great diorite statue formerly stood in it. It has, however, been set exactly twenty-five pyramid inches (cubit) from the centre of the chamber passing through the apex of its inclined roof-stones, thereby defining––as was first suggested by Piazzi Smyth––the standard of the architect's longer unit of measure, the pyramid cubit (refer p. 18 above).

The Grand Gallery is the most imposing structure in the Great Pyramid, being twenty-eight feet high, or seven times the height of the Ascending Passage leading to it, a contrast that makes it all the more impressive. It is just over 150 feet long up to the Great Step at its upper end, but barely seven feet wide between its walls, and only half this between the ramps running its full length at their base, and terminating in the face of the Step, which extends from wall to wall.

A unique feature of the Gallery's construction is the manner in which each course of its walls is offset from the one below—or overlaps—so that the topmost courses come sufficiently close together to enable the Gallery to be roofed with a single row of stones like the key-stone of an arch. The method of construction, in fact, is analogous to that of an arch, but simpler and better adapted to the peculiar conditions involved.

The Great Step, which is now much dilapidated, though approximately a yard high, is not intended to denote that measure as has been often asserted by pyramid writers and students. Our yard is far too empirical a measure to be incorporated in such a scientific structure as the Great Pyramid.

This step leads to a low passage, just over four feet long, built through the south end wall of the Gallery, which in turn gives access to the Ante-chamber, nine feet eight inches in length and five feet across above the wainscot, by twelve and a half feet high ; but barely two feet inside this chamber a granite leaf, or portcullis, is met with, which reduces the head-room again to that of the passage from the Gallery.

This portcullis, which consists of two stones, one above the other, was first called a "leaf" by Prof. Greaves, from its similarity to the "leaf" or sliding door in a river or canal lock-gate, and this description has clung to it ever since. Although it fits into grooves in each wall of the chamber, it is not a true portcullis, since it rests at the bottom on the walls themselves, the grooves not being carried down to the floor, so that it is not capable of being lowered. (Diagram p. 81.)

On the upper stone of this leaf is a small projecting boss, exactly one pyramid inch in thickness, and like a horse-shoe in shape. It has been formed by dressing down the *whole* of this face of the portcullis, both top and bottom stones— not only the one on which it is formed—to the extent of one inch. The labour thus involved indicates it fulfils an important function, and was not formed merely for lifting the block into position, as often maintained. Examination shows that this boss is a standard measure of the Pyramid's smallest unit of length—the inch ; for, in addition to being exactly that amount in thickness, it is also set one inch eccentric in the granite leaf, being that amount from the true centre thereof measured from one wall of the Ante-chamber to the other (this eccentricity was first noticed by Professor Smyth, and has been verified by later investigators) ; while its lower edge is five inches above the joint between the upper and lower stones composing the Granite Leaf, indicating a fifth part of the pyramid cubit.

Connecting the Ante-chamber to the King's Chamber is another passage similar to that between the Gallery and Ante-chamber, but just twice the length, generally referred to as the Second Low Passage.

The King's Chamber is a noble apartment, measuring thirty-four feet long (east to west) by seventeen feet wide and nineteen feet high. Its walls are built of exactly one hundred stones of varying size, while its ceiling is formed of nine immense granite beams, each weighing an average of fifty to sixty tons, while the largest, measuring twenty-seven feet by seven feet by five feet, is estimated to be nearly seventy tons in weight.

Above this ceiling is a series of spaces or "construction chambers" as they are called, each roofed in with similar huge beams extending up to the true topmost gabled roof. Their purpose is to act as a "shock-absorbing" device to protect the main chamber below from being crushed as a result of earthquake shock or subsidence, and to relieve it of the great weight of superincumbent masonry rising to the apex.

The Coffer, or chest, in the King's Chamber, though called a sarcophagus by those regarding the Pyramid as a tomb, and though prepared for a lid as all true sarcophagi have, exhibits none of the hieroglyphics or other markings found on sarcophagi, the apparent preparation for a lid (the existence of which has never been known) being another instance of a *blind*, purposely done to deceive, and to give the idea of a mausoleum to the Great Pyramid. This coffer is a lidless stone box, intended as a measure of capacity, and contains exactly four British quarters of wheat—the old Anglo-Saxon "chaldron"—additional evidence of the connection of the Great Pyramid with ourselves.

It is also interesting to note that the Ark of the Covenant, if the cubit of Ex. xxxvii, 1 be taken as the pyramid cubit—which is undoubtedly the same as the sacred Bible cubit used by Moses and Solomon—had virtually the same cubic capacity as this coffer. Its dimensions (see Ex. xxxvii, 1, 6) were two and a half cubits long, one and a half broad, and one and a half high, these being the *outside* measurements, since, for one thing, its vertical measurement is called the height and not its depth. Also the mercy-seat, forming the lid of the Ark, is given as of the same length and breadth (2½ × 1½ cubits) as the Ark itself; these therefore were the overall dimensions. Reduced to pyramid inches its dimensions were 62½ × 37½ × 37½.

Assuming the ends and sides were one and three-quarter inches thick and the bottom two inches—a fair proportion considering its size, the material used (wood) and the weight carried in it (see I Kings viii, 9)—its cubic capacity would be 71,213 pyramid inches compared to 71,317 for the coffer in the Pyramid (see p. 163 of Smyth's *Our Inheritance*, 4th ed.). Seeing that the coffer is much damaged, making exact measurements difficult, and has been hand-worked out of a very hard material, this close agreement is remarkable, and is sufficient to show the *intention* of absolute equal capacity, which cannot be mere coincidence.

This coffer has been worked out with bronze tools from a single block of red granite, hollowed out by drilling and chiselling, the marks of the tools being still visible.

The secret which the ancient Egyptians possessed of working extremely hard substances such as would have turned the edge of steel cutting tools—like quartz and diorite—has apparently very recently been discovered. A new alloy of copper and beryllium (less than 2¼ per cent) with the qualities of steel was shown at an engineering exhibition in New York during December, 1932. An excess of beryllium renders the alloy too hard to work.

ASTRONOMICAL FEATURES

One of the earliest facts discovered in connection with the astronomical features of the Great Pyramid was that the entrance passage, round about the year 2140 B.C., pointed in the direction of the then pole star, which at that date was the star *Alpha* in the constellation of the Dragon. This condition could also apply to the year 3434 B.C. (See Frontispiece.)

When this particular feature was first noted by Sir John Herschel in the early part of last century, Egyptologists inferred he was maintaining that the Great Pyramid had been originally intended as an astronomical observatory, but since this was clearly impossible, they argued this discovery was merely a coincidence, ignoring the fact that Sir John never made such a claim for the Pyramid, but that it did intend to *monumentalize* this fact for the purpose of exact chronology. The year thus indicated he calculated as approximately 2160 B.C. ; while Piazzi Smyth, some thirty years later, gave it as 2170 B.C., and at the same time discovered that the scored line in the entrance passage, if produced as a perpendicular thereto, pointed in the direction of the star *eta* (or *Alcyone*) in the constellation of the Pleiades. That is to say, when *alpha Draconis* shone down the passage, *Alcyone* was at the same time on a meridian due south, thus indicating a particular astronomical conjunction which cannot happen again till after the lapse of 25,827 years, owing to what is known as Precession of the Equinoxes.

This is a very slow motion of the earth—the cumulative effect of various influences—which causes the poles to alter the direction in which they point to the heavens, the effect of which causes the sun to arrive at the equinoxes a fraction earlier each year; hence the term *pre*-cession of the equinoxes.

Not only was the fact of Precession known to the builder of the Great Pyramid, but also its value, yet its computation has only been arrived at really accurately during this century. This value is given by the sum of the two diagonals (AC and DB in diagram at p. 27) of the Pyramid's square base expressed in inches, and equals 25,826.54, a figure also found in the measure of the Pyramid's perimeter at the level of the King's Chamber, on the fiftieth masonry course, which may thus be defined as the Precessional circuit of the Great Pyramid. The Great Pyramid, therefore, may be considered the earliest known record in existence wherein is embodied the fact of the immense cycle known as Precession of the Equinoxes.

Owing to the extremely slow movement of this cycle, it is obvious that the position of the then pole star would appear to be the same for a great many years. Hence the reason for the architect defining the particular conjunction of *alpha Draconis* and *Alcyone* by means of the scored line, thereby defining a precise date for purposes of exact chronology—midnight of autumnal equinox of 2144 B.C., according to modern astronomical computation.

It does not necessarily follow, however, as Piazzi Smyth and other investigators have thought, that this date was the year of the Pyramid's completion. All available evidence (discussed at length at pp. 10-21 *Mystery of the Great Pyramid*) indicates it was constructed considerably earlier, while there seems little doubt that the year of the Pyramid's completion was originally defined by the position of the entrance door in the north face as 2625 B.C., a date which fell within the reign of Khufu.

The particular astronomical feature thus embodied in the alignment of the Great Pyramid's entrance passage, in conjunction with the scored line therein, was not therefore intended for contemporary purposes, as has generally been hitherto assumed, nor had it any special significance for that era. Its purpose is to supply a datum for pyramid chronology by fixing midnight as the zero for day reckoning, and its year as commencing at the autumnal equinox, because this particular conjunction could only have taken place in the year indicated at that particular point of time.

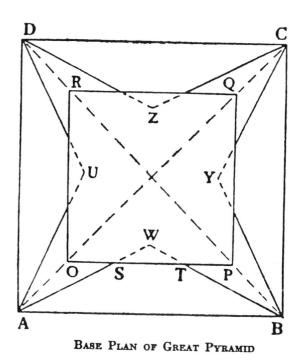

BASE PLAN OF GREAT PYRAMID

The Great Pyramid also defines the different year-values in which the annual orbit of the earth can be expressed. These different values arise from the fact that the inclination of the earth's axis of rotation is neither constant in amount nor direction, and that its plane of revolution is not rigidly fixed. They are geometrically defined in the pyramid's base plan as follows :—

1. The *recessed* circuit, ASTB, etc., on scale of 100

inches to the day, gives the mean value of the *sidereal* year=365.2564 days.*

2. The true *square* circuit, ABCD, gives the mean length of the *solar* (or tropical) year=365.2424 days.

3. The *geometrical* circuit, AWBYC, etc., defines the *anomalistic* (or orbital) year=365.2599 days.

These values are defined in the Great Pyramid with an accuracy only arrived at by modern computation, and exhibit an astronomical knowledge much in advance of the ancient Greek astronomers.

The base plan of the pyramid also gives the earth's mean distance from the sun as 92,996,085 miles, but as the explanation and computation are somewhat involved, the reader is referred to our larger work for details (pp. 111-116, *Witness of the Great Pyramid*, 2nd Ed.).

---

* A fuller definition of these different year-values, given for the benefit of the non-astronomical reader, may be stated as follows :

1. The *Sidereal* year is the interval between the Earth's position *at any time* relative to the fixed stars, and its next return to that same position.

2. The *Solar* year is the interval between successive equinoxes—autumn or spring—or between successive solstices—summer or winter.

3. The *Anomalistic* year is the interval between the Earth's successive annual returns to the point in its orbit at which it most nearly approaches the Sun, usually described as Perihelion, and occurs on January 2-3. It is then computed to be distant 91,838,000 miles from the Sun.

Of these the Solar year is the shortest, and the Anomalistic the longest, the difference being approximately 24½ minutes.

CHAPTER III

THE GREAT PYRAMID'S CHART OF WORLD-HISTORY

REMARKABLE as are the foregoing scientific facts embodied in the structure of the Great Pyramid, the most interesting feature for the student of prophecy is that its passages and chambers enshrine a chronologic record of 6,000 years of human history in the form of a chart or diagram, the structural changes in these passages defining the dates of epoch-making events throughout that record, the time measurement of which is an inch to a year.

This chronologic theory first occurred to John Taylor, a pioneer in Great Pyramid investigation, to test which was largely the object of Piazzi Smyth's survey of the pyramid. Noticing that the length of the Ascending Passage, from its junction with the Entrance Passage up to the Grand Gallery, corresponded in inches to the number of years from the Exodus to the time of our Lord, Taylor concluded that herein lay the hidden purpose of these passages—a chart of world-history.

It was another investigator, Robert Menzies, of Leith, who suggested to Smyth that the astronomical date defined by the alignment of the Entrance Passage on to the Pole Star would also be marked—if Smyth's calculation was correct—in the passage itself. This suggestion led to the discovery of the "scored lines" referred to above, and the fact that the date so defined is now taken to be 2144 B.C., instead of Smyth's 2170 B.C., is due to the fact that Smyth, as a pioneer, had insufficient data to guide him, and had also to work from a more or less arbitrarily-chosen basal date, selecting the junction of the Ascending Passage and

Grand Gallery as a datum, reckoning this as the Nativity in A.D. 1 (in itself an error of four years), and working back from that point till he reached the scored line. In addition, his results were based on the tape measure, which cannot give the necessary accuracy, as the true geometrical basis of the pyramid's representation—which alone can produce the accuracy required—had not then been discovered.

The zero point of the pyramid's chronology is obtained by the intersection of the *roof* line (not floor line, as often stated) of the Ascending Passage produced backwards with the face of the pyramid similarly produced, and a perpendicular therefrom to the floor line. This gives the year (autumn equinox) 4000 B.C. as the basal date, and the beginning of Adamic history, precisely as derived from Bible chronology.* (See frontispiece.)

The terminal point of this chronology is given by producing the gallery floor-line (SR) to meet the vertical centre-line of Portcullis at point T : the date so defined is autumn equinox A.D. 2001, thus completing the 6,000 years of the Pyramid's chronograph, and synchronizing with the similar period of Bible history and prophecy.

Reference to frontispiece will show how outstanding dates in world-history are defined by notable structural changes : the *Exodus* (1486 B.C.) where the Ascending Passage commences ; the *Nativity* (4 B.C.), by the point where the floor-line of the Queen's (properly the Jews') chamber produced backwards meets the floor of Ascending Passage ; the *Crucifixion* (A.D. 30), by junction of roof line of Ascending Passage with north wall of Gallery, and a perpendicular therefrom to the floor. At this point the roof of the Gallery is raised, or "lifted up," 286.1 inches (the Pyramid's "displacement factor") above that of the Ascending Passage leading to it, thus symbolizing our

---

* Refer author's *True Bible Chronology* (Routledge), showing synchronization of Pyramid and Bible chronology, and the universal nature of the basal date of all chronology when properly derived.

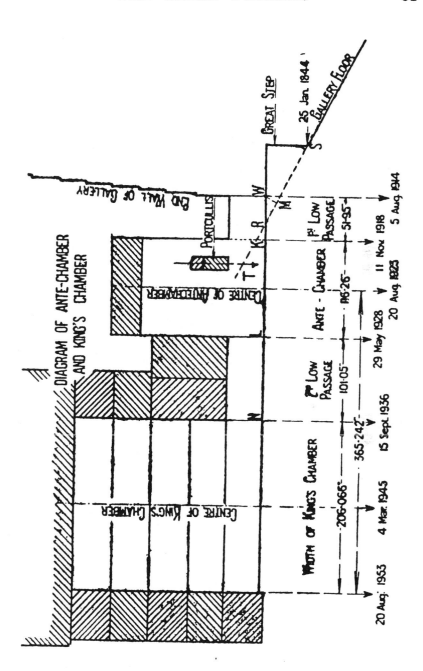

Lord's words, "I, if I be *lifted up* from the earth, will draw all men unto Me. This He said, signifying what death He should die" (John xii, 32-3). The Grand Gallery thus fitly symbolizes by its loftiness the Gospel era inaugurated by our Lord's Death and Passion.

The next date defined is that marked by the **Great Step**—January 25th, 1844—one of importance astronomically in the Pyramid's representation of chronology, the explanation of which is given in our larger work, but is somewhat too technical and involved to explain in this introductory essay.

The breaking of continuity of the Gallery floor at this point, and the change of direction to the horizontal, implies a change of chronologic scale—a change first suggested by the late William Reeves, of Toronto, in the early part of this century—the rate for this level portion being an inch to a *month*; not our varying month of thirty or thirty-one days (since a varying unit cannot be geometrically represented by a fixed one—an inch), but the ancient Egyptian and Biblical month of thirty days.

That a new scale is here introduced is also indicated by the fact that the Ante-Chamber and King's Chamber extend *beyond* the Portcullis which marks—as explained above—the termination of the general inch-year scale, the two scales being geometrically connected in order to maintain the necessary continuity between them,* and also to define the basal date of the larger scale as August 5th, 1914, which is given by the point M on the inch-year scale, and by the point W on inch-month scale.

This enlarged scale is defined in the Pyramid itself. From the centre of the Ante-Chamber to the south wall of the King's Chamber is a distance of 365.242 inches, equivalent to the number of days in a solar year. This distance is

---

* Many attempt to establish this continuity by measuring *up* the face of the Step and *then* along the horizontal, oblivious of the fact that it is geometrically incorrect to run two different scales into one another, and that one *must not go round corners.*

the circumferential measure of a circle whose diameter equals the length of the Ante-Chamber (116.26 inches)—one instance of the use of the year-circle referred to above. The number 365.242 is therefore symbolic, and signifies a great year of 365.242 months, each of thirty days, exactly equivalent to 360 of our *varying* months (10,957.26 days). To find equivalent dates in our calendar, therefore, calculations must be reduced to a common denomination of *days*. The period thus included is therefore precisely one of thirty solar years—August 20th, 1923, to August 20th, 1953.

The Great Pyramid embodies two separate systems of chronology : a *General System*, on a scale of one Pyramid inch to a solar year; and a *Special System*, applying only to modern times, on an enlarged scale of one Pyramid inch to a month, covering the period from August 2nd, 1909—the date equivalent to the commencement of the level floor line at top of Great Step—to August 20th, 1953, where it terminates in the opposite wall of the King's Chamber. The Pyramid's passage system, in fact, is analogous to the working drawings of some engineering undertaking. There is the general drawing showing the whole scheme on a small scale, while separate portions are given on an enlarged scale to show the details of construction for the contractor to carry them out.

Not only is the scale thus enlarged to show the greater detail of modern history, but there is also a clear distinction involved between these two representations. As already pointed out, the message of the Great Pyramid is specifically addressed to modern times. That is to say, its general, small-scale, system was intended to be studied, and its significance understood with respect to *past* history, during the era defined by its special, larger-scale, system—the opening years of the twentieth century. And such precisely has been the case.

The first Low Passage defined precisely the duration of

the late war, from August 5th, 1914, to November 11th, 1918; that is, from the time of our entry into it until the armistice. The reason why the date of *our* participation in the late war is given, rather than the actual date of its commencement (July 28th), is because this level portion constitutes—to use an engineering term—*our* "working drawings" as the great Architect's contractors building up His Kingdom on earth. August 5th, 1914, is therefore defined as a critical date in modern times and a turning point in recent history, the beginning of a period of trial for the "builders."

The open space of the Ante-Chamber represents a period of truce in tribulation, due to Divine intervention, and symbolizes the "shortening" of Matt. xxiv, 22, introduced into what otherwise would have been a *continuous* period of trial extending from August 5th, 1914, to September 15th, 1936, this latter date being defined by the entrance to the King's Chamber. To introduce this shortening, as has been proposed, by altering the scale for the Second Low Passage to an inch for a *week* is contrary to the laws of geometrical representation. *One must not alter the scale of representation in the middle of the diagram.*

The granite Portcullis in the Ante-Chamber, temporarily reducing the headroom again to that of the Low Passage, symbolizes the unrest, social and industrial, which was such a universal feature immediately following the arti- ficially-produced post-war boom.

This truce ended on May 29th—30th, 1928, when the Second Low Passage was entered, representing another period of trial for the "builders." The different nature of this second phase—financial, economic, and political— such as the writer indicated previous to May, 1928, would probably be the case (refer. p. 221, *Witness of the Great Pyramid*, 2nd Ed.), is suggested by the different material (granite) through which the Second Low Passage is carried. The first one being in limestone—a poor material to resist crushing—signified a period of trial of a severe *physical* nature and under conditions ill-fitted to survive it. Hence the chaotic condition in all spheres of our civilization following the cessation of hostilities in the late war.

The period of truce given by the Ante-Chamber was one of warning respecting the nature of the tribulation to follow in the Second Low Passage, by noting what occurred on the various dates defined in it, particularly by the three Portcullis Grooves (see p. 41). It was thus that the above forecast suggested itself to the writer.

It was also suggested by the events that transpired while we were passing under the Granite Leaf or Portcullis— social and industrial trouble. Being a representation, on a very reduced scale in length, of the Second Passage also in *granite*, it indicated similar chaos, but of deeper and wider incidence, during the passage of the latter. History since May 1928, has amply verified this.

Few to day will dispute the fact that, since the summer of 1928, we have been passing through an extremely critical period, in some rexpects even more critical than at the crisis of the late war,* and it was on May 29th, 1928, that the various factors, economic and industrial, which have since developed into this crisis, now involving the whole world, first began to reveal themselves. This crisis is indicated as continuing till September 15th, 1936.†

There is the following remarkable fact respecting the two low passages symbolizing periods of stress. Their combined length is exactly 153 inches—the number of fishes Peter drew to land in the miraculous haul in the sea of Tiberias

* "We are under the shadow of the most ominous economic crisis that has ever afflicted the world in times of peace. . . . There is nothing less than a world, nothing less than a system, which is crumbling beneath our feet."—The Prime Minister at the Lausanne International Conference (1932).

† The reader is recommended to read pp. 35-62 of the author's *At Midnight a Cry!* (Covenant Publishing Co., Ltd.) wherein the features and progress of the present world-crisis are dealt with at greater length than is possible here, and the probable outcome of it.

(John xxi, 11).   In Matt. xiii, 47-9, is a parable giving this incident in parable form, wherein Christ likens the good fish, gathered safely to land, to the just, whom the angels separate from the wicked, who are the bad fish cast back into the sea—ending with the words : "So shall it be at the end of the age."   The number 153 is thus here connected with the "elect," for whose sake these days are shortened (insertion of Ante-Chamber), and identifies the Great Pyramid's symbolic prophecy with our Lord's prophecy concerning the final tribulation which was to precede His Second Coming.

The King's Chamber, to which the Second Low Passage leads, symbolizes the Judgment Hall of the Nations, and the *preparation* for our Lord's rule on earth, the period represented by its width being the *initial* stage of real world-reconstruction—September 15th, 1936, to August 20th, 1953.

It may be asked why the chronology terminates at August 20th, 1953, instead of being carried on to finish at the opening of the Millennium in A.D. 2001, but is apparently broken off abruptly.   This is explained as follows :—

As already pointed out, this enlarged chronologic system represented by the two low passages, ante-chamber and King's Chamber, constitutes the "working drawings" of the British Race as the Great Architect's builders on earth. This is shown by the fact that they are set out in our unit of measure—the inch, and August 20th, 1953, is the limiting date for their application, though the contract itself must be completed by September 15th, 1936, the final date of the great "Seven Times"—but *may* be completed earlier. That is to say, responsibility is taken out of our hands after August, 1953, and vested solely in the Architect.

The King's Chamber represents the preliminary readjust-
ment of this world's affairs preparatory to the real work of
reconstruction, and it is during this preliminary period
that the "builders," in whom this process of restitution
is first effected (by virtue of the circumstances of the final
tribulation compelling them to call upon the Architect "to
do it for them" (Ezek. xxxvi, 37)—that is, complete their
contract—thus shortening their own tribulation), are pro-
tected from the effects of the drastic changes which will be
wrought upon the Gentile nations of the world, such pro-
tection being symbolized by the so-called construction-
chambers above the King's Chamber, which protect it from
the effects of subsidence and other damage.

Such is the symbolism of the King's Chamber respecting
the years preceding the establishment of the Millennium,
and such is portrayed in Isaiah xxvi, 16-21. That is to say,
actual work of world-reconstruction does not begin till
after August 20th, 1953, and is completed by A.D. 2001,
when the Millennium sets in.

This preparatory period is defined in prophecy as the
era of the "cleansing of the Sanctuary" in Dan. viii, 14,—the
"restitution of all things," of Acts iii, 21, itself immediately
preceded by the "period of the Consummation" of Dan. ix,
27 (1891-1936), when all these things shall be finished.
(Refer. pp. 76-7 of the author's *Times of the Gentiles.*)

The symbolism indicates that the dominance of the
present evil forces in the world—the "unclean spirits" of
Rev. xvi, 13—is ended by September 16th, 1936, and mankind is completely purged of their power by August 20th,
1953. The period of forty-eight years thence to A.D. 2001
denotes a second and more advanced stage of the cleansing,
restoration, and re-organisation—spiritually, morally and
physically—which the whole world will have to undergo in
order to fit it for the ideal conditions of Christ's Millennial
reign.

SYMBOLISM OF THE GREAT PYRAMID

These passages are not only a diagrammatic forecast of world-history, but have also a symbolic significance as well. Thus the Descending Passage, with its very restricted head-room, typifies the steady descent of the human race in spiritual degradation, this decline being arrested for the moment at the point where the Ascending Passage comes in, which symbolizes a spiritual *ascent*, but still in a cramped space, typifying the restricted conditions imposed by the "yoke of the law."

Continued decline is indicated by the descending passage being carried on, past the Ascending Passage, in a steadily downward direction, till it ultimately finishes in a subterranean pit, with very chaotic floor but smooth ceiling, symbolizing a state of spiritual chaos, or upside-down-ness, an arresting symbol of the bottomless pit of the Apocalypse.

This subterranean pit is itself symbolic of the pit out of which come "the three unclean spirits like frogs," which are steadily and insistently intensifying this state of chaos until it finally resolves itself into the climax of Armageddon. No intelligent observer can fail to see how the whole world, particularly the Far East, is falling under the malign influence—in greater or less degree—of the forces of chaos led by Bolshevism.

While the subterranean passages and chamber of the Great Pyramid indicate evil influences, its upper and ascending passages symbolize the effects of Divine influence and the rise to better things. Thus the Ascending Passage, which appropriately commences at the date of the Exodus, denotes the call of the Israelites when they were taken out from the nations of the world to be the witnesses of a higher religion, and the means of the ultimate redemption of all mankind. The nation Israel (the "building-race" of Pyramid prophecy—in modern times, Britain) is thus represented as progressing "under the Law," towards the

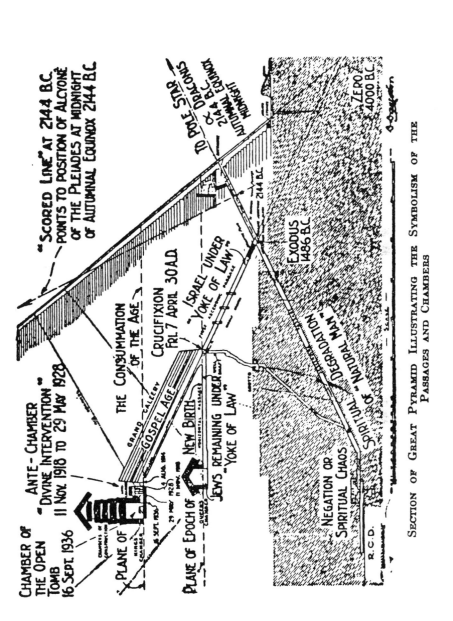

SECTION OF GREAT PYRAMID ILLUSTRATING THE SYMBOLISM OF THE PASSAGES AND CHAMBERS

time and condition when the True Light would come to lighten that darkness (John viii, 12 ; xii, 35, 46). This is confirmed in the Egyptian texts where this Passage is described as the "Hall of Truth in *Darkness*" (see *Mystery of the Great Pyramid*, pp. 90-92), in distinction to the "Hall of Truth in *Light*," or Grand Gallery, which by its loftiness aptly typifies the Light of the Gospel Age.

The Horizontal Passage, taken off at junction of Ascending Passage and Grand Gallery, since it denotes the date of the coming of Messiah, appropriately marks the plane of the epoch of spiritual re-birth, or second birth (the Second Adam). Though the Jews were offered to partake of the privileges thereby inaugurated, they rejected them, thereby remaining under the yoke of the Law, indicated by this passage's continued restricted head-room.

The symbolism of the Ante-Chamber as a period of shortening of tribulation has already been explained. It thus supplies a period of warning regarding the nature of events dominating the second phase of tribulation indicated by the Second Low Passage. Herein lies the significance of the three portcullis grooves in this Chamber, which Egyptologists are unable—as in other details of the Great Pyramid—to account for except on grounds which are untenable (see *Witness of the Great Pyramid*, pp. 157-8). These grooves *symbolize* the position of three successive veils or screens, thus implying that the Ante-Chamber represents a period of unveiling previous to a resumption of tribulation, a symbolism confirmed by its allegorical significance (see *Mystery of the Great Pyramid*, pp. 100-102). That is to say, the events which took place on the particular dates defined by the centre of each groove—that is, as we successively passed through each veil—indicated by their nature what we might expect would develop after we entered the Second Low Passage. The reliability of the Great Pyramid's forecast has been vindicated in no uncertain fashion (see p. 35 above), particularly in its warn-

ing, given by the great earthquake in Palestine and Trans-
jordania on July 11, 1927, the date defined by the centre
of its last Portcullis Groove (E in diagram), that abnormal
natural phenomena and other disasters would be an accom-
paniment of economic distress throughout the world.

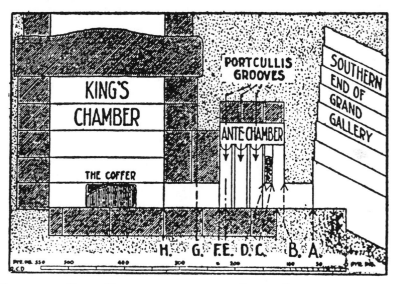

SECTION OF GREAT PYRAMID FROM TOP OF GRAND GALLERY INTO KING'S
CHAMBER, SHOWING PORTCULLIS GROOVES IN ANTE-CHAMBER

Our Lord also has told us that, at the time of the end,
mankind would be warned by previous events as to the
nature of future events. This is precisely the sequence of
warning and future effect given by the Pyramid's Ante-
Chamber. It likewise uttered the warning "Watch !"

Had this warning been heeded, we should not have had
the exaggerated, and often wild, prognostications made in
the popular press by irresponsible journalists and others
about the Great Pyramid and May 29th, 1928, which
were naturally seized upon to discredit the whole subject.
Time, however, quickly proved the folly of jumping
to conclusions, a step the writer, for one, always warned
against. It is to be hoped that similar foolishness will not

be indulged in as we approach the Pyramid's next out-standing date—Sept. 15th, 1936 (H in diagram)—but wait till it arrives. Also, do not *necessarily* expect something spectacular, and remember its significance may not appear till it has passed. (Regarding the possible connection of this date with events leading to the Second Advent, see *At Midnight a Cry* !, Ch. vii, and pp. 143-5.)

CHAPTER IV

THE MISSING APEX-STONE OF THE GREAT PYRAMID

A PECULIARITY of the Great Pyramid, and one which makes it conspicuous amongst its neighbours, in addition to its great size, is its truncated summit. From the fact that this peculiarity, giving it the appearance of incompletion, is confined to the Great Pyramid, it is generally assumed that it was originally built with its summit rising to an apex, and that its present blunted appearance is due either to earthquake damage, or to deliberate spoliation such as has led to the loss of its casing-stones.

When, however, we remember the symbolic nature of the Great Pyramid, and the specific references to it in Scripture, and that it is the only form of building which answers to the description of that spiritual building of which Christ is spoken of as "chief corner-stone and headstone of the corner" (Ps. cxviii, 22 ; 1 Pet. ii, 7), a reason at once suggests itself for its missing top-stone. For only in the top-stone of a pyramid can a corner-stone be at the same time a headstone or cap, wherein all its four sides meet ; a two-fold condition which cannot be fulfilled in any other form of building. And even as Christ, the spiritual headstone of Scripture, is yet absent from us in Body and invisible, so, too, is the Pyramid's headstone, which typifies Messiah, missing, rejected by the builders, even as Christ was rejected of men (Isaiah liii, 8).

This allegorical significance of the Pyramid's top-stone has been denied by some in their attempts to belittle the whole subject, by quoting Isai. xxviii, 16, where this same "stone" is referred to as a "*foundation* stone." This, how-ever, has reference to Messiah as His first Advent. To Israel at His Second Coming He becomes "the headstone of the corner" (Zech. iv, 7). This allegory has yet to be fulfilled both symbolically (when the Pyramid will be com-pleted by the placing in position of its top-stone) and actually at the Second Coming. Then shall we see fulfilled the words of Matt. xxi, 42 : "The stone (Christ) which the builders rejected, the same is become the head of the corner" —referred to by St. Peter in Acts iv, 11 : "This (Christ) is the stone which was set at naught of you builders, which is become the head of the corner."

Herein is revealed the meaning of the allegory of the "Stone Kingdom" of Daniel (ii, 45), of which the Great Pyramid is the counterpart and "witness in stone," and of which Christ is chief corner-stone. By our Lord's own testimony this "stone" kingdom is a NATION—not a church such as our theologians suppose it to be—that has supplanted the Jewish race, which, according to St. Peter, would become the "builders," and eventually fill the whole earth. The Great Pyramid identifies this nation as the British Race, since its allegory is specifically addressed to it (refer Ch. II above), while that Race *alone* fulfils *all* the marks of identification Daniel has described as charac-teristic of the "Stone" kingdom of prophecy.

In virtue of this allegory attached to the Great Pyramid and its top-stone, the present writer has always been of the opinion that the top-stone has been missing from the beginning, rejected by the builders for some reason or another, or, as has also been suggested, not completed owing to the difficulty of the task, a fact which would not be surprising when we consider the constructional and mechanical problems to be solved, in conjunction with its size : over forty-eight feet wide at the base, and about thirty feet high—a no mean pyramid in itself. Writers, too, from the earliest times—Greek, Roman, and Arab—have all invariably commented upon the truncated appearance of the Great Pyramid. By such rejection the builders, *unwittingly*, carried out the allegory when erecting their allegorical structure.

This inference now appears to have been proved correct, as the result of a survey carried out by the Egyptian Government during 1925-6.* In the course of this survey fragments of casing-stones were found in locations widely apart (between SO and TP) in line with those already discovered many years ago at the centre of the base-side (as at ST, see diagram at p. 27), set back, or recessed, from the outer square, ABCD, defined by the corner-sockets.

This means that the Pyramid was actually constructed on the base OPQR, instead of on the *designed* base ABCD. Actually the error is so small—infinitesimal in proportion to the size of the structure (the amount of recessing being but thirty-six inches in a total length of over 750 feet)— that only very careful instrumental observation would detect it at all. These features must of necessity be greatly exaggerated in any diagram to make them clear to the reader.

The casing-stones were intended to take the line ASTB, etc., thus following the form of the inner core masonry, this peculiar shape of which is distinctly seen in a remarkable air photograph published by Mr. Davidson in one of his *Morning Post* articles (taken by Brigadier-General Groves, C.B., D.S.O.)—also in his article in the *Structural Engineer* of March, 1930.

That the casing-stones are now proved to have been set out on the recessed square throughout its *whole* length, O to P, confirms Petrie's reconstruction showing them thinner

* *Determination of the Exact Size and Orientation of the Great Pyramid of Giza*, by J. H. Cole, B.A., F.R.G.S. (Government Publications Office, Cairo). (*Survey of Egypt*. Paper No. 89.)

at the corners than at the centre. Had they been uniform throughout, the completed structure would have stood over the base ABCD.

The casing *as built*, therefore, did not precisely define by the base-plan the year-values given above (p. 28), but details of construction, as revealed by the corner sockets and the geometrical lay-out, clearly prove it was intended to do so. It should be remembered that the whole basis of the Great Pyramid is *geometry*, which alone will reveal the true intention of its architect.

The result is shown to be, then, that the Pyramid's *actual* base square circuit is *less*, by the value of its "*Displacement Factor*" (286.1 py. ins.), than the theoretically correct—and *intended*—square circuit of 36,524.2 inches; or 36,524.2 less 286.1. This gives a circuit of 36,238.1 py. inches (or 36,277.8 British ins.), the equivalent value of the figure given in the above survey.

To carry out the correct angle of slope from base to summit, means that this error was introduced throughout the whole structure, so that the circuit *at any level* was 286.1 inches short of the true circuit according to the design for that circuit. This means that the platform for the top-stone was itself too small, so that the stone was rejected. The "Displacement" allegory was thus embodied in the actual work of construction.

Now the circuit of the platform intended for the apex-stone measures *seven* times 286.1 Pyramid inches, or seven times its displacement factor, whereas it should measure *eight* times that value. Dr. Bullinger, author of *Numbers in Scripture*, and an authority on Bible numerics, points out that *seven* denotes completion, while *eight* "is *over and above this perfect completion*" ... "the number specially associated with the *beginning of a new era or order*," and such is precisely what the coming of Messiah will inaugurate. Eight is thus specially associated with Christ (His Name, Jesus, in Greek, adds up to 888), and is therefore fitly symbolized in the apex-stone of the Great Pyramid, itself the symbol of Messiah.

Thus does the Pyramid's *eight* times displacement in *design* of its perfect apex-stone, fitly symbolize that perfect structure described in Ephes. ii, 19-21. For until this "headstone of the corner" has been lifted up, the building cannot be perfected.

St. Paul tells us : "Ye are built upon the foundation of the apostles and prophets, *Jesus Christ Himself being the chief corner-stone;* in whom all the building fitly framed together groweth unto an holy temple in the Lord." Does not the allegory fitly express such a building as herein described by St. Paul as a counterpart of that spiritual building of which Christ is the Head ? And does not the apex-stone of a pyramid "fitly frame together the whole building," while lacking it is incomplete ?

The fact that the apex-stone of the Great Pyramid is missing lends peculiar interest and significance to the design of the original seal of the United States of America, adopted in 1782, for the reverse side of this seal is a representation of the Great Pyramid with its top-stone missing, but suspended above it under the eye of Providence. Seeing how much the Great Pyramid is bound up with Anglo-Saxon history and purpose, this adoption of it as a seal by the Manasseh branch, at a time, too, when its significance was hardly even suspected, is truly remarkable, and is one of those instances of blind and unconscious testimony to the (generally) unrealized facts of our true origin which so often come to light.

GREAT PYRAMID ON SEAL OF U.S.A.

CHAPTER V

WHO BUILT THE GREAT PYRAMID?

APART from the many speculations that have been made as to the purpose of the Great Pyramid, the question as to who erected it is almost as speculative, and at least as interesting a one to ask. It is a question that has been addressed to the writer by many enquirers.

Though the name of Khufu has always been attached to it, and while his name—and that of his successor, Khafra—appears on the ceiling-beams of the King's Chamber, he is not even traditionally associated with its erection as the actual architect. The evidence of his cartouche therein merely shows it was completed within his reign, and therefore could not have been intended as his tomb, as all access to the King's Chamber was prevented as soon as it had been roofed in ; that is, while Khufu was still alive. Khufu was merely enlisted, along with his subjects, in supplying the organization and labour necessary for its construction, such being under the control and supervision of a few highly-skilled supervisors *belonging to another race*, Asiatic or Arabian in origin.

The foreign origin of the builder is not only upheld by traditions preserved by Manetho, Herodotus, Diodorus and Josephus, who assert the Great and Second Pyramids were erected under the supervision of members of an immigrant race who entered Egypt peaceably, but also by the following considerations :—(i) The use of measures unknown to the ancient Egyptians (see ch. ii) ; (ii) the scientific and mathematical knowledge incorporated in the Great Pyramid, also unknown to the Egyptians ; and (iii) the extreme

48

accuracy of the workmanship due to instruction under highly skilled supervisors.

On this latter point, Sir Flinders Petrie, referring to the era of the Great Pyramid builders, remarks : "The exquisite workmanship [not only in the Pyramid but in other contemporary structures] did not so much depend upon a large school of widespread ability, *as upon a few men far above their fellows.*" And referring specifically to the Great Pyramid, he says :—"The supreme accuracy was *limited to the skill of ONE man.*" (our italics.)

Amongst the various individuals that have been suggested as this one individual—Seth, Enoch, or Shem—it is the last-named that has generally been fixed upon as the actual architect of the Great Pyramid.

The solution of this problem, however (that is, of course, as far as such is possible), depends upon a careful co-ordination of all the data we have bearing upon the matter, and if such co-ordination be made, it will be discovered that, from the chronological data alone—Egyptological, Biblical, and from other sources—neither of these three suggested names could have been responsible for the Great Pyramid, and certainly not Shem, the one most commonly associated with it.*

Egyptological evidence (refer Davidson's *Early Egypt,* Chart 1) fixes the *sole* reign of Khufu as extending from

---

* Mr. Davidson has made the following very true observation : "The science of co-ordination teaches us to recognize obstacles for what they are *by taking in* the general aspect of *the whole field of vision. It surprises me the number of people who cannot co-ordinate ;* who trip over obstacles, and fail to progress through trying to remove such obstacles." (*National Message,* 27-11-26)—(our emphasis). This inability to co-ordinate, even by some calling themselves scientific, is a trait which has likewise frequently caused surprise to the present writer, and is mainly the reason for the parrot-like repetition of errors by one author after another so often met with, and common in Great Pyramid literature. In fact, it was this unscientific method so apparent in books thereon that started him originally to study the Great Pyramid and test for himself the (often contradictory) statements made, mathematically and scientifically. Writers will not, as a rule, "take in the whole field of vision," but only that restricted portion of it which suits their particular theories on the subject.

2645 to 2622 B.C.—twenty-three years (confirmed by Professor Langdon fixing date of Menes of the First Dynasty at 3100 B.C. by astronomical data).

Coptic tradition says preliminary work on the Pyramid was begun during the reign of Shaaru (Surid) while co-rex with Seneferu (last king of third dynasty), actual construction commencing with Khufu on death of Seneferu and while Surid was still alive, in 2645 B.C. Now Herodotus tells us actual construction occupied twenty years, so that the Pyramid was completed in 2625 B.C., *precisely the date indicated in the structure itself* (refer p. 26 above). Incidentally, the fact that preliminary work and actual construction extended throughout four overlapping reigns —Seneferu, Shaaru, Khufu and Khafra (the latter being co-regent with Khufu at the time)—proves none of these was the actual architect.

Further, Coptic tradition also asserts the Great Pyramid was begun 300 years before the Deluge : this visitation fell in 2344 B.C., according to Biblical chronology giving the same basal date (4000 B.C.) as the Pyramid's chronograph. Here again we have chronological agreement. Co-ordination thus definitely fixes the era of the Great Pyramid's construction as lying between 2645 and 2625 B.C., agreeable to the known reign of Khufu.

Now this era does *not* correspond with any years falling within the dynasties of either Seth, 3870-2958 B.C. ; Enoch, 3378-3013 B.C. ; or Shem, 2441-1841 B.C. ; the first two being long before the time of the Pyramid, while Shem comes at least 200 years *afterwards.** The Great Pyramid era falls within that of the dynasty of Noah, 2944-1994 B.C.

Seth has been given as the builder on the strength of Josephus, who, however, states that "the *descendants* of Seth [not Seth himself], after perfecting their study of

* These dates for Seth, Enoch and Shem are obtained from the same data that fixes the Deluge at 2344 B.C., as above. Refer the writer's *True Bible Chronology* for details.

astronomy, set out for Egypt and there embodied their discoveries in the building of two 'pillars' (*cf.* Isai. xix, 19, =
monuments), one of stone and the other of brick, in order
that this knowledge might not be lost before they were
sufficiently known, upon Adam's prediction that the world
was to be destroyed by a flood," thereby confirming the
pre-deluge date for the Great Pyramid. (See *Antiquities*,
bk. i, Ch. iii).

The writer is of opinion that the actual architect was a
member of the Melchisedec order of priest-kings ; not the
one recorded in Gen. xiv, 18, but an *earlier* member thereof.
And in this connection there is the Egyptian tradition
which attributes the design of the Great Pyramid to
Iemhotep, architect to King Zoser of the Third Dynasty
(2707-2688 B.C.),* and also states that the plans of it
"descended to him from heaven" (Weigall); in other words,
that the Great Pyramid was divinely inspired (refer p. 9
above). Now, according to Sir Wallis Budge, the name
Iemhotep has the same meaning as the Hebrew Melchisedec
—"king of peace," or righteousness, a fact which lends a
strong probability to the identification of the Great
Pyramid's architect with this character.

Bearing also in mind the allegorical significance of the
Great Pyramid as typical of the Messianic Kingdom, of
which Christ, "priest for ever after the order of Melchisedec,"† is the Head and chief Corner-stone, it would be
quite fitting that its architect was a member of this order

* Hence the experimental pyramids of Zoser and Seneferu, during whose
reign preliminary work on the Great Pyramid was carried out, referred to
above in our first chapter (p. 5).

† Note that the name is used with reference to an *order* or dynasty, not a
particular individual, borne by each representative thereof—a dynasty of
Priest-kings, and of a higher order than the Aaronic line (Heb. vii, 11).
The somewhat mysterious reference in Heb. vii, 3, which has puzzled
everyone to explain, simply means that this dynasty existed by right of
virtue, rather than by descent from father to son. Melchisedec is here
referred to as "*like unto* the Son of God" ; not Christ Himself, but as a *type*,
and therefore a *man*, of whom St. Paul adds, "Consider how great this *man*
was." It represented the highest order of earthly priest-kings as a type of
Christ the highest of all (Heb. vi, 20).

of Adamic priesthood. Such an origin, also, would explain why the paganism of Egypt was suppressed during the construction of the Great and Second Pyramids, and why these two structures *alone* are totally free ot hieroglyphics and pictures such as are found on all purely Egyptian edifices.

It would also account for the peaceable subjection of the country, since such presupposes exceptional moral influence, so that a mere handful of colonists were able to induce Egypt and its rulers to close the temples and cast out their heathen gods "without a battle" (as Manetho tells us), and to lend their co-operation in raising an imperishable monument to the true God.

A common error, also, based upon statements made by Manetho and Herodotus, who have mixed up their history, is to identify this race of colonists with the so-called Hyksos, or Shepherd kings of Egypt. Herodotus in particular is very untrustworthy, as is shown, for example, by his placing the Great Pyramid builders of the IVth dynasty *after* Rameses III of the XXth, some fourteen centuries later!

This confusion arises from treating *similar* circumstances as if they were *identical,* a mistake made by the late Piazzi Smyth, Col. Garnier, and many others before and since. Like the Pyramid builders, the Hyksos also suppressed the native religion, but for very different reasons. The former were also very likely shepherds as were the later Hyksos invaders, whose coming into Egypt was very largely a case of history repeating itself from the time of Khufu and Khafra.

A little co-ordination, however, will show how impossible it is for the Hyksos dynasty of the Egyptologists to have been responsible for the Great and Second Pyramids. This dynasty arrived in Egypt 1937 B.C., contemporary with the close of the twelfth native Egyptian dynasty, and lasted till 1830 B.C., or *practically seven centuries after* the time of the Pyramid builders. In fact, the twelfth dynasty saw the end of all pyramid building in Egypt (refer p. 8 above).

Co-ordination, therefore, of all available evidence leads to the conclusion that the Great Pyramid was erected by a band of colonists, probably from Asia or Arabia, belonging to the Adamic race, very highly developed and of exceptional moral and intellectual attainments, but who kept their knowledge secret. These colonists, forewarned of the calamity later to overwhelm their civilization in the land of its origin—Central Asia—were divinely directed to Egypt, there to set up this "pillar to the Lord," not only as a memorial to the scientific achievements of that now dead civilization, but as a message and a warning to one then unborn.

This message is purposely intended for the present crisis, addressed to a race in need of spiritual revival, such as even the trial of the late war failed to bring about. And to call forth this revival, we are being taught that reliance on things material is of little avail, for it is upon the material assets of our civilization that attack is being made. All systems, political, religious, financial and economic, are to-day being tested in the furnace of adversity. In putting *material* interests first, we have forgotten the *spiritual*. "Seek ye *first* the Kingdom of God," was our Lord's injunction, and material blessings will follow (Matt. vi, 33). We are to-day learning what little value material things have when we forget the Kingdom of God, which St. John tells us can only be entered by the new birth. It is to compel us as a nation to seek this new birth spiritually that this distress is being visited upon us.

The symbolism of the Great Pyramid shows that we shall emerge safely from our present trials after seeking Divine aid, and that that aid will be given, *perhaps* when little expected, even as the crisis of the late war came to a sudden and unexpected ending.   We must remember, however, that by ourselves we can do nothing. It is because man has been attempting, by his own initiative and by his own methods, to straighten out the chaos which the late world-war has bequeathed us, that that chaos is to-day far worse, and will continue to deepen so long as such methods are persisted in.   Seeking Divine aid and asking God to "do it for us" will alone find the solution.

"Except the Lord build the house, they labour in vain that build it ; except the Lord keep the city, the watch-man waketh but in vain" (Psalm cxxvii, 1).

FINIS

INDEX

Alcyone and *Alpha Draconis,* 25
Apex-Stone of G.P., 43-47
Ark of the Covenant and Pyramid's Coffer, 24
Astronomical Features of G.P., 25-28

Builders of the G.P., 8, 48-53

Cubit (Pyramid), 13, 21, 24

Dahshur, Pyramids of, 4, 6, 7
Dates defined in G.P.:
  4000 B.C., 30
  2625 B.C., 26, 50
  2144 B.C., 26, 29
  1486 B.C., 30
  4 B.C., 80
  A.D. 30, 30
  A.D. 1844 (Jan. 25), 82
  A.D. 1909 (Aug. 2), 83
  A.D. 1914 (Aug. 5), 32, 84
  A.D. 1918 (Nov. 11), 84
  A.D. 1923 (Aug. 20), 83
  A.D. 1927 (July 11), 41
  A.D. 1928 (May 29), 84, 35, 41
  A.D. 1936 (Sept. 15), 84, 35, 86, 42
  A.D. 1945 (March 4), 31
  A.D. 1953 (Aug. 20), 83, 86
  A.D. 2001, 30, 86
"Displacement Factor" of G.P., 19, 80, 46

Early Pyramid Building, 5, 18
Egyptologists and the G.P., 2, 40
Equinox (Precession of), 25-26

GREAT PYRAMID (*see* PYRAMID)

Herschel (Sir John), astronomer, 25
Hyksos Dynasty, 52

Inch (British and Pyramid), 13, 22

Knufu (or Cheops), 26, 48, 49

Meidoum Pyramid (Seneferu's), 4, 6

Orbit of Earth defined in G.P., 14, 27-28

Petrie (Sir F.), Egyptologist, 6, 7, 12, 17, 45, 49
Pyramid-building, Era of, 8
PYRAMID (THE GREAT):
  Allegory of, 15, 43-47
  Ante-Chamber, 22, 82, 34, 35, 40
  Apex-Stone, 43-47
  Base as *Designed* and as *Built,* 45-46

PYRAMID (THE GREAT) : *continued*
  Bible References to, 10
  Boss on Granite Leaf, 22
  "Building-Race" of, 15, 34, 36, 88, 44
  Casing Stones, 17, 45
  Chronologic Record of, 29, 33
  Coffer in King's Chamber, 23-24
  "Construction Chambers," 23, 37
  Date of Completion, 26, 50
  Divinely Inspired, 8, 9, 51
  First Low Passage, 22, 33
  Forced Entry into, 2, 19
  Geographical Position of, viii, 10
  Geometrical Basis of, 12, 46
  Grand Gallery, 21, 30, 32, 40
  Granite Leaf or Portcullis, 22, 80, 34, 35
  Granite Plug, 2
  Great Step, 22
  King's Chamber, 23, 82, 36, 87
  Not of Egyptian Origin, 3
  Origin of Name, 19
  Passage System of, 19-21
  Pavement Round, 18
  "Precession" defined in, 26
  Problem of, 3
  Purpose of, 4, 8
  Queen's Chamber, 21, 30
  Scientific elements in, 8
  "Scored Lines" in, 25, 29
  Second Low Passage, 23, 34, 85, 40
  Subterranean Pit, 20
  Sundial (use as), 18
  Symbolism of, 37, 38-42
  Workmanship of, 17

Sakkara Pyramid (Zoser's), 4, 5
Seal of U.S.A., 47
Second (Khafra's) Pyramid, 3, 6, 7, 19, 48
Smyth (Piazzi), astronomer, 11, 23, 25, 26, 29
"Squaring the Circle," 16
"Stone Kingdom" of Daniel, 44
Stonehenge, 15
Sun's mean distance, 28

Tombic Theory of G.P., 2, 5
Taylor (John), Pyramid Investigator, 29

Yard (British), not in G.P., 22
"Year-Circle" in G.P., 15, 83

Zoser's Pyramid, 4, 5, 51 (*f.*)

55

BOOKS ON THE GREAT PYRAMID BY THE SAME AUTHOR

THE WITNESS OF THE GREAT PYRAMID. Demy 8vo., 292 pp., Second Edition. Illustrated.

An exposition of every branch of learning concerning the Great Pyramid, written for the non-technical reader. An outstanding *popular* work on a subject of wide interest. Mr. Davidson says of it: "A most clearly-written and comprehensive exposition. . . . A work of this nature has long been needed." Another reader says: "Your book is the clearest I know of on the subject."

THE MYSTERY OF THE GREAT PYRAMID. Demy 8vo., 150 pp., Illustrated.

Explains in detail the close affinity between the Egyptian "Book of the Dead" and the Great Pyramid, and the Messianism revealed in both—corrupted in the "Book of the Dead," but truly given in the Pyramid. Gives also much information regarding Pyramid traditions on the structure and its builders.

"Your reputation will be enhanced by this book, *which fills in many gaps and is absorbingly interesting.*"—F.W.

BY GEORGE R. RIFFERT

GREAT PYRAMID PROOF OF GOD. Demy 8vo., 226 pp., Illustrated.

Extract from Preface: "This book commemorates three things: a crisis period in world affairs and religion; the increasing significant message of the Great Pyramid; and last, just another effort, urgent, honest, and, we hope, helpful, to enlighten and inspire such as may be interested. . . . Presents all the facts which the greatest living authorities on the Pyramid confirm, and should be of value and interest to layman and learned alike."

OTHER SUN BOOKS TITLES
you may find of interest:

AMERICAN INDIANS

BENEATH THE MOON AND UNDER THE SUN: A Re-Appraisal of the Sacred Calendar and the Prophecies of Ancient Mexico by Tony Shearer. The Sacred Twins, Tezcatlipoca - The Dark Lord, The Symbolic Glyphs, The 13 Sacred Numbers, The Dark House, Quetzalcoatl, The Prophecies Unfold, The Ceremony.

ASTROLOGY

ALAN LEO'S DICTIONARY OF ASTROLOGY by Alan Leo. Aaron's rod, Casting the Horoscope, Disposition, Ecliptic, Equinoxes, Period of the Sun, Objects Governed by Planets, Mean Time, Etc.

THE ASTROLOGICAL GUIDE TO HEALTH FOR EACH OF THE TWELVE SUN SIGNS by Ariel Gordon, M.C. Information regarding the twelve signs of the Zodiac is taken from seven of the greatest authorities, past and present, on the different correspondences, as well as from personal experience, extending over many years of private practice.

ASTROLOGICAL INVESTIGATIONS by W. Frankland. Importance of Correct Time, Judgement, Type of Horoscope, Examples of Areas. Birth Numbers, The Point of Life, Age Along the Zodiac, Ponderous Planets, The Moon's Nodes, Transits. Etc.

ASTROLOGICAL PREDICTION by P. J. Harwood. Place and Time in Different Parts of the World, Erecting Horoscopes, Astrological Predictions, Transits and Various Directions, Life Periods, The Radical Horoscope, Marriage, Travel, Change and General Fortune, Time of Action, Horoscopical Studies of Famous Individuals, Etc.

ASTROLOGY: HOW TO MAKE AND READ YOUR OWN HOROSCOPE by Sepharial. The Alphabet of the Heavens, The Construction of a Horoscope, How to Read the Horoscope, The Stars in Their Courses.

ASTROLOGY IN RELATION TO MIND AND CHARACTER by A Mental Specialist. Reading the Sample Map, The Cusps of the Horoscope, Character, The Balanced vs Unbalanced Mind, Suicidal Tendencies, A Case of Panic Treatment, Heredity, Etc.

A BEGINNER'S GUIDE TO PRACTICAL ASTROLOGY by Vivian E. Robson. How to Cast a Horoscope, Planets, Signs, and Houses, How to Judge a Horoscope, How to Calculate Future Influences, etc.

BIBLE ASTROLOGY by Lyman E. Stowe. Astrology and Phrenology, More Than One Zodiac, The Earth's Change of Poles Brings Floods, The Pyramids, The Zodiac on the Human Hand. The Symbols of All Religions, The Origin of the Easter Festival, Reincarnation in the Bible, Stories of the Bible Made Plain by Astrology, The Twelve Signs of Jacob, The Riddle of the Sphinx, When Aquarius Begins to Reign, Freemasonry and Astrology, The Evolution of the Bible, Astrology as a Science, Etc.

THE BOWL OF HEAVEN by Evangeline Adams. My Job and How I Do It, A Tale of Two Cities, "Dabbling in Heathenism", We are All Children of the Stars, Life and Death, The Money-Makers, Some Ladies of Venus, I Never Gamble, A World in Love, Astrological Marriages. The New Natology, Twins and Things, Am I Always Right?

THE COSMIC KEY OF LIFE SELF-REALIZATION by A.S. Vickers. The Cosmic Key of Life, Selecting a Goal, Concentration, What is a Science? Key to Horoscope Blanks, Horoscopes of Noted Persons, Planetary Positions, Planetary Aspects, Sign Keywords, Astrological Attributes. Etc.

DIRECTIONAL ASTROLOGY by Sepharial. Astronomical Definitions, Example Horoscope, Directions in Mundo and the Zodiac, Order and Effects of Directing, Planetary Indicators, Ptolemy and Placidus, Poles and Fortune, Lunar Equations, True Directing, Various sets of Tables.

THE EARTH IN THE HEAVENS - RULING DEGREES OF CITIES - HOW TO FIND AND USE THEM by L. Edward Johndro. Precession, Midheavens and Ascendants, Calculating Midheavens and Ascendants, Use of Locality Angles, Verification by World Events, Applications to Nativities.

ECLIPSES IN THEORY AND PRACTICE by Sepharial. The Natural Cause of an Eclipse, Eclipses of the Sun, Lunar Eclipses, To Calculate an Eclipse, Eclipse Signs, Eclipse Indications, The Decanates, Transits over Eclipse Points, Individuals and Eclipses, Illustrations, Etc.

FIRST PRINCIPLES OF ASTROLOGY by Wilber Gaston. The Zodiac and It's Signs, The Signs Interpreted, The Cusps, Planetary Influences, Astrology and Heredity, Forming the Horoscope, Index to Characteristics, Etc.

THE FIXED STARS AND CONSTELLATIONS IN ASTROLOGY by Vivian E. Robson. The Fixed Stars in Astronomy, Natal and Mundane Astrology, The Influence of the Constellations, The Lunar Mansions, Nebulae and Clusters, Stars and Constellations in Mediaeval Magic, The Fixed Stars in Astro-Meteorology, Mathematical Formulae.

HEBREW ASTROLOGY by Sepharial. Chaldean Astronomy, Time and Its Measures, The Signs of the Zodiac, How to Set a Horoscope, The Seven Times, Modern Predictions.

THE INFLUENCE OF THE ZODIAC UPON HUMAN LIFE by Eleanor Kirk. The Quickening Spirit, Questions and Answers, Disease, Development, A Warning, Marriage, The Fire, Air, Earth and Water Triplicities, Etc. (This is an excellent book!)

THE LAW OF VALUES by Sepharial. General Principles, Planetary Values, Effects of Transits and Aspects, Sensitive Points, How to Invest, How to Average, Etc.

THE LIGHT OF EGYPT or THE SCIENCE OF THE SOUL AND THE STARS by Thomas H. Burgoyne. Vol.1: Realms of Spirit and Matter, Mysteries of Sex, Incarnation and Re-Incarnation, Karma, Mediumship, Soul Knowledge, Mortality and Immortality. Basic Principles of Celestial Science, Stellar Influence on Humanity, Alchemical Nature of Man, Union of Soul and Stars. Vol. II: The Zodiac and the Constellations, Spiritual Interpretation of the Zodiac, Astro-Theology and Astro-Mythology, Symbolism and Alchemy, Talismans and Ceremonial Magic, Tablets of AEth including: The Twelve Mansions, The Ten Planetary Rulers, The Ten Great Powers of the Universe, and Penetralia - The Secret of the Soul.

MANUAL OF ASTROLOGY by Sepharial. Language of the Heavens, Divisions of the Zodiac, Planets, Houses, Aspects, Calculation of the Horoscope, Measure of Time, Law of Sex, Hindu Astrology, Progressive Horoscope, Etc.

MEDICAL ASTROLOGY by Henrich Däath. Anatomical Sign-Rulership, Planetary Powers and Principles, Biodynamic Actions, How the Planets Crystallize in Organic and Inorganic Life, Zodiaco-Planetary Synopsis of Typical Diseases, Gauging Planetary Strengths in the Specific Horoscope, Application, Examples, Indications of Short Life. Etc.

NEW DICTIONARY OF ASTROLOGY In Which All Technical and Abstruse Terms Used In The Text Books of the Science Are Intimately Explained And Illustrated by Sepharial. Everything from Abscission to Zuriel.

NEW MEASURES IN ASTROLOGY, A Symbolic Basis in Directions by W. Frankland. Directions, House Division, House influence, Planets and Signs, The Measure and its Symbolism, The Measure and Examples, The Scope of Nativity, Horoscope: A Key to Development.

THE PLANETS THROUGH THE SIGNS: Astrology for Living by Abbe Bassett. Includes chapters on the Sun, Moon, and various planets, and how each one influences us through the different signs of the Zodiac.

PRIMARY DIRECTIONS MADE EASY by Sepharial. Principles of Directing, Polar Elevations, Illustrations, Mundane Aspects, Zodiacal Parallels, Mundane Parallels, Suggested Method, The Telescopic View, Solar and Lunar Horoscopes, Etc.

PROGNOSTIC ASTRONOMY, The Scientific Basis of Astrology by Sepharial. The Use of an Ephemeris, Primary, Mundane and Zodiacal Directions, Aspects and Parallels in Mundo, Conjunctions and Aspects in the Zodiac, Effects of Directions, The Part of Fortune, The Houses of the Heavens, Lunar Parallax and Equation, Etc.

RAPHAEL'S GUIDE TO ASTROLOGY by Raphael. Symbols Explained, Nature of Aspects, Signs, Orbits of Planets, Persons Produced by the Signs, Form of Body, How to Erect a Map, Place Planets, The Term Elevation, How to Judge a Nativity, Health, Money, Employment, Travel, Etc., On Selection of a House, Friends and Enemies, Calculating Future Events, Returns, Transits, Eclipses, A Short Astrological Dictionary, Etc.

RAPHAEL'S KEY TO ASTROLOGY by Raphael. Planetary Aspects and Orbs, Description of Persons Produced by the Signs, Use of an Ephemeris, How to Erect a Map of the Heavens, Influence of Planets, How to Judge a Nativity, Whether a Child Will Live or Die, Health and Mental Qualities, Money, Employment, Marriage, Children, Travel, Friends, Enemies, Kind of Death, Etc.

RAPHAEL'S MEDICAL ASTROLOGY or the Effects of the Planets on the Human Body by Raphael. Zodiac and Human Body, Planetary Rulership and Action, Health and Constitution, Physical Condition, Duration of Life, Examples of Early Death, Diseases, Mental Disorders, Injuries, Accidents, Deformities, Health and the Horoscope, Preventive Measures, Herbal Remedies, the Course of Disease, Astrology and Colors, Etc.

RAPHAEL'S MUNDANE ASTROLOGY or The Effects of the Planets and Signs Upon the Nations and Countries of the World by Raphael. Mundane Astrology, Planetary and Zodiacal Signs and Symbols, The Twelve Mundane Houses, Significations of Planets, Essential and Accidental Dignities, Mundane Map, Concerning Houses and Planets, How to Judge a Mundane Map, Ellipses, Earthquakes, Comets, Planetary Conjunctions, Parts of the World Affected by Signs of Zodiac. Etc.

THE "REASON WHY" IN ASTROLOGY or Philosophy and First Principles by H. S. Green. The Solar System, Two Zodiacs, Three Circles and Four Points, The States of Consciousness, Twelve Signs and Houses, Planets and / in Signs, Earth's Magnetism, The Five Planets, Three Worlds, Gunas and Elements.

RELATION OF THE MINERAL SALTS OF THE BODY TO THE SIGNS OF THE ZODIAC by Dr. George W. Carey. Biochemistry, Esoteric Chemistry, Twelve Cell-Salts of the Zodiac, Etc.

THE RISING ZODIACAL SIGN: Its Meaning and Prognostics by Coulson Turnbull. How To Determine the Rising Sign, Tables I, II, and III.

THE SCIENCE OF FOREKNOWLEDGE AND THE RADIX SYSTEM by Sepharial. Science of Foreknowledge, Astrology in Shakespeare, Celestial Dynamics, Neptune, Astrology of Lilith, Indian and Hebrew Astrology, Joan of Arc, Methods of Ptolemy and Benatti, Radix System, Horoscopical Anomalies, Our Solar System, Financial Astrology.

THE SILVER KEY: A GUIDE TO SPECULATIONS by Sepharial. The Future Method, Science of Numbers, Finding the Winner, The Lunar Key, Gravity and Evolution, Something to Come, A Warning, On Speculation, Monte Carlo and Astrology, Tables of Sidereal Times, Tables of Ascendants, Etc.

SOLAR BIOLOGY by Hiral E. Butler. Bible History of Solar Biology, Involution and Evolution, Man's True Nature, The Selection of Partners and Hints Regarding Marriage, The Twelve Signs or Functions of the Zodiac, The Power and Importance of Breath, The Polarities of the Signs, Order and Harmony of the Seven Vital Signs, The Positions of the Planets, Attributes of Character, Critical Periods of Life, Sexual Excesses, Etc.

THE SOLAR EPOCH - A NEW ASTROLOGICAL THESIS by Sepharial. The History of Birth, The Lunar Horoscope, The Solar Horoscope, Directional Influences, Conclusions.

THE SOLAR LOGOS or Studies in Arcane Mysticism by Coulson Turnbull. Logos, Kingdom of the Soul, Intuition and Motion, Mystic Macrocosm, Spirit of the Planets, Mystical Sun and Moon, Soul in Action, Spiritual Horoscope, Health, Disease, Service, Etc.

THE STARS - HOW AND WHERE THEY INFLUENCE by L. Edward Johndro. Astronomical Fundamentals, Application of Fixed Stars to Nativities and Mundane Astrology, Verification by Nativities, Verification by World Events, Variable Stars, Binary Stars, Double Stars, Clusters, Nebulae and Bright Stars, Etc.

A STUDENTS' TEXT-BOOK OF ASTROLOGY by Vivian E. Robson. Fundamental Principles of Astrology, Casting the Horoscope, Character and Mind, Occupation and Position, Parents, Relatives and Home, Love and Marriage, Esoteric Astrology, Adoption of the New Style Calendar.

WHAT IS ASTROLOGY? by Colin Bennett. How an Astrologer Works, Sign Meanings, How Aspects Affect a Horoscope, Numerology as an Astrological Aid, Psychology In Relation to Astrology, Etc.

WHEN WERE YOU BORN? by Cheiro. Characteristics of Persons Born in Each Month of the Year as well as chapters on the Occult Significance of Numbers with Birth Dates, Life's Triangles and Affinities, and Lucky Colors and How to Know Them.

ATLANTIS / LEMURIA

ATLANTIS IN AMERICA by Lewis Spence. Atlantis and Antillia, Cro-Magnons of America. Quetzalcoatl the Atlantean, Atlantis in American Tradition and Religion. Ethnological Evidence, Art and Architecture, Folk-Memories of an Atlantic Continent, Analogy of Lemuria. Chronological Table, Etc.

THE PROBLEM OF LEMURIA - THE SUNKEN CONTINENT OF THE PACIFIC by Lewis Spence, Illustrated. Legend of Lemuria, Argument From Archaeology, Testimony of Tradition, Evidence from Myth and Magic, Races of Lemuria, Testimony of Custom, Proof of Art, Geology of Lemuria, Evidence from Biology, Catastrophe and its Results, Life and Civilization in Lemuria, Atlantis and Lemuria, Conclusions.

SEMA-KANDA: THRESHOLD MEMORIES by Coulson Turnbull. Ra-Om-Ar and Sema-Kanda, The Brotherhood, The Scroll, Posidona, Ramantha's Lesson, The Great White Lodge, The Destruction of Atlantis, The Two Prisoners, The Congregation of the Inquisition, The Horoscope, Etc.

WISDOM FROM ATLANTIS by Ruth B. Drown. Being, Divine Selfishness, Service, Nobility of Self-Reliance, Harmony, Divine Love, Principles of Life and Living, Man's Divine Nature, Faith, True Thinking.

AUTOSUGGESTION / HYPNOTISM

AUTO-SUGGESTION: WHAT IT IS AND HOW TO USE IT FOR HEALTH, HAPPINESS AND SUCCESS by Herbert A. Parkyn. M.D. C.M. Auto-suggestion - What it is and how to use it, Its effects and how to employ it to overcome physical and mental troubles, Auto-suggestion for the formation of character and habits, Personal magnetism, Cultivation of optimism, Developing concentration, Achievement of success, Breathing exercises, Influence on health in Winter, Diagnosis and treatment of typical case of chronic physical suffering, Auto-suggestion basis of all healing, How psychic pictures are made realities.

CHRISTIANITY AND AUTOSUGGESTION by C. Harry Brooks and Rev. Ernest Charles. Autosuggestion and the Teachings of Christ, Faith and Autosuggestion. The Power Within, God and the Unconscious, Christian Specific Suggestion, Temptation, Etc.

EMILE COUÉ: THE MAN AND HIS WORK by Hugh MacNaughten. Author's Notes, Nancy or London, M Coué at Eton and London, The Sub-Conscious Self, On Some Stumbling Blocks, M Coué in His Relation To Christianity, On "Everything for Nothing", M. Coué, Envoi, Etc.

HOW TO PRACTICE SUGGESTION AND AUTOSUGGESTION by Emile Coué, Preface by Charles Baudouin. Interviews of Patients, Examples of the Power of Suggestion and Autosuggestion, Suggestions: General and Special, Suggestions for Each Ailment, Advice to Patients, Lectures Delivered by Emile Coué in America.

HYPNOTISM AND SELF-EDUCATION by A. M. Hutchison M.D. History of Hypnotism, Methods of Inducing Hypnosis, Theories and Phenomena of Hypnotism, Suggestion, Self-Suggestions, Medical Treatment, Education of Children and of Oneself, Etc.

MY METHOD by Emile Coué. Chapters include: Autosuggestion Disconcerting in its Simplicity, Slaves of Suggestion and Masters of Ourselves, Dominance of Imagination over Will, Moral Factor in all Disease, Don't Concentrate, How to Banish Pain, Psychic Culture as Necessary as Physical, Self-Mastery Means Health, Etc.

THE PRACTICE OF AUTOSUGGESTION BY THE METHOD OF EMILE COUÉ by C. Harry Brooks. The Clinic of Emile Coué, A Few of Coué's Cures, Thought is a Force, Thought and the Will, The General Formula, How to Deal With Pain, Autosuggestion and the Child, Particular Suggestions, Etc.

SELF MASTERY THROUGH CONSCIOUS AUTOSUGGESTION by Emile Coué. Self Mastery Through Autosuggestion, Thoughts and Precepts, What Autosuggestion Can Do, Education as it Ought to Be, A Survey of the "Seances", the Miracle Within, Everything for Everyone, Etc.

SUGGESTION by Edward B. Warman A.M. Faith - An Essential Element, Psychotherapy, Thought - An Origin of Disease, Adverse Suggestions, Cast Out Fear, Power of Thought in Autosuggestion, Suggestions To and For Mothers, For Children Backward in Studies, Suggestion as an Educator, Why Repeat Suggestions, A Few Experiences in Healing, Etc.

SUGGESTION AND AUTOSUGGESTION by Charles Baudouin. Why Do We Ignore Autosuggestion? Representative, Affective, Motor, Conditional Suggestions, The Action of Sleep, The Law of Reversed Effort, Relaxation and Collectedness, Autohypnosis, Moral Energy, Exercises, Coué's Practice, Acceptivity and Suggestibility, The Education of Children, Methods of Application,

CLAIRVOYANCE

CLAIRVOYANCE AND CLAIRAUDIENCE, PREMONITIONS AND IMPRESSIONS by Edward B. Warman, A.M. Clairvoyance or Telepathy, Does the Soul Leave the Body, A Word of Warning, Clairaudience, Premonitions and Impressions, A Premonition Foretold to Skeptics, Lincoln's Premonition, The "Still Small Voice."

SECOND SIGHT - A STUDY OF NATURAL AND INDUCED CLAIRVOYANCE by Sepharial. The Scientific Position, Materials and Conditions, The Faculty of Seership, Preliminaries and Practice, Kinds of Visions, Obstacles and Clairvoyance, Symbolism, Allied Psychic Phases, Experience and Use.

CONSPIRACY

THE ILLUMINOIDS - SECRET SOCIETIES AND POLITICAL PARANOIA by Neal Wilgus. Detailed picture of Weishaupt's Order of the Illuminati as well as other secret societies throughout history. Ties various far-reaching areas together including important information relating to the J.F. Kennedy assassination. "The best single reference on the Illuminati in fact and legendry" - Robert Anton Wilson in Cosmic Trigger.

COOKBOOKS

VEGETARIAN MENUES, One For Each Day in a Month, 185 Recipies Arranged and Compiled by Clara Louise Bemister. These menues were first published in *New India*, they are now put in book form, hoping they will help those desirous of eating pure food.

CRYSTALS/MINERALS

CRYSTALS AND THEIR USE—A Study of At-One-Ment with the Mineral Kingdom by Page Bryant. Mineral Consciousness, Crystals and Their Use, Sacred Centers, Various Types of Crystals, The Amethyst, Crystal Gazing.

THE MAGIC OF MINERALS by Page Bryant. Inner Lives of Mineral Kingdom, Megalithic Mysteries and Native American View, Healing Properties of Minerals, Psychic Influences in Minerals, Stones of the Zodiac, Crystals and Their Use, General Information on Selection, Use, and Care of Minerals.

4

MAN, MINERALS, AND MASTERS by Charles W. Littlefield, M.D. School of the Magi, Three Masters, The Cubes, Initiation in Tibet, Hindustan, and Egypt, History, Prophecy, Numerology, Perfection.

PLANETARY INFLUENCES AND THERAPEUTIC USES OF PRECIOUS STONES by George Frederick Kunz. Includes various lists and illustrations, Etc.

DREAMS

DREAMS: WHAT THEY ARE AND WHAT THEY MEAN, by J. W. Wickwar. Dreams: Through the Ages, Dreaming and Sleeping, The Dream: A Theory, Dreams: Their Cause and Make-Up, Day Dreams, Prophecies, etc., Reflection and Wireless, Psycho-Analysis, The Dream Complex, Custom, Superstition, and Belief. "The Meaning of Dreams."

DREAMS AND PREMONITIONS by L.W. Rogers. Introduction, The Dreamer, The Materialistic Hypotheses Inadequate, Dreams of Discovery, Varieties of Dreams, Memories of Astral Experiences, Help from the Invisibles, Premonitory Dreams, Dreams of the Dead, How to Remember Dreams.

THE MEANING OF DREAMS by Isador H. Coriat M.D. The Problem of Dreams, An Example of Dream-Analysis, Dreams as the Fulfillment of Wishes, The Unconscious, The Mechinism and Function of Dreams, Dreams of Children, Typical, Prophetic, and Artifical Dreams, Dreams and Nervous Diseases.

THE NATIONAL DREAM BOOK by Claire Rougemont. Clairvoyance, Explanation of Dreams and Visions, Air and Celestial Fire, Water and Navagation, Land, Flowers, Herbs, Grains, Trees, Birds, Insects, Reptiles, Fish, Childbirth, Various Human Body Parts, Garments and Apparel, Singing and Musical Instruments, Games, Drunkards, Running, Funerals and Death, Religious Matters, Celestial Bodies, Alphabetical List of Dreams, Etc.

EARTH CHANGES (Also See Prophecy)

CHEIRO'S WORLD PREDICTIONS by Cheiro. Fate of Nations, British Empire in its World Aspect, Destiny of the United States, Future of the Jews, Coming War of Wars, Coming Aquarian Age, Precession of the Equinoxes.

THE COMING STAR-SHIFT AND MANY PROPHECIES OF BIBLE AND PYRAMID FULFILLED by O. Gordon Pickett. God Corrects His Clock in the Stars, Joseph Builder of the Great Pyramid, Numerical Harmony, Prophecy, World Wars, Star-Shifts, The Flood, Astronomy, The Great Pyramids, Etc.

COMING WORLD CHANGES by H.A. and F.H.Curtiss. The Prophecies, Geological Considerations, Philosophy of Planetary Changes, King of the World, Heart of the World, Battle of Armageddon, The Remedy.

EARTH CHANGES NOW! by Page Bryant. The Earth is Changing: The Evidence, We Knew it was Coming!, The Sacred Covenant, Externalization of Spiritual Hierarchy, Earth Angel: A Promise for the Future.

THE EARTH CHANGES SURVIVAL HANDBOOK by Page Bryant. The Emergence of Planetary Intelligence, Mapping the Earth, Earth Changes: Past and Future, Preparing for the Future. Walking in Balance, Etc. (Our Second Best Selling Title!)

ORACLES OF NOSTRADAMUS by Charles A. Ward. Life of Nostradamus, Preface to Prophecies, Epistle to Henry II, Magic, Historic Fragments, Etc.

PROPHECIES OF GREAT WORLD CHANGES compiled by George B. Brownell. World-War Prophecies, Coming Changes of Great Magnitude, False Christs, The New Heaven and the New Earth, The New Order and the Old, Etc.

ROLLING THUNDER: THE COMING EARTH CHANGES by J. R. Jochmans. The Coming Famine and Earth Movements, The Destruction of California and New York, Future War, Nostradamus, Bible, Edgar Cayce, Coming Avatars, Pyramid Prophecy, Weather, Coming False Religion and the Antichrist, and much, much more! This book is our all-time best seller!

UTOPIA II: AN INVESTIGATION INTO THE KINGDOM OF GOD by John Schmidt. Why Utopia?, Mankind's Past, Present and Future, A Sociological Look, A Political Look, An Economic Look, A Spiritual Look.

EGYPTOLOGY

THE MYSTERIES OF EGYPT or The Secret Rites and Traditions of the Nile by Lewis Spence. Orgin and Philosophy of the Mysteries, Mysteries in Other Lands, The Ritual Rebirth and Reconstruction of the Mysteries, Illusion and Phantasmagoria, Temples and Sites, The Survival of the Mysteries, The Significance of Initiation.

GENERAL METAPHYSICAL

THE CABALA - ITS INFLUENCE ON JUDAISM AND CHRISTIANITY by Bernard Pick. Name and Origin of Cabala, Development of Cabala in Pre-Zohar Period, Book of Zohar or Splendor, Cabala in the Post Zohar Period, Most Important Doctrines of Cabala, Cabala in Relation to Judaism and Christianity.

COSMIC CONSCIOUSNESS by Ali Nomad. Man's Relation to God and His Fellow Man, Areas of

Consciousness, Instances of Illumination and its After Effects, Examples of Cosmic Consciousness, Moses, Gautama, Jesus, Paul of Tarsus, Mohammed, Emanuel Swedenborg, Modern Examples of Intellectual Cosmic Consciousness: Emerson, Tolstoi, Balzac, Methods of Attainment: The Way of Illumination, Etc.

EPISODES FROM AN UNWRITTEN HISTORY by Claude Bragdon. H.P.B. and Her Adept Teacher, Olcott, Early Days of the Theosophical Society, Judge, Sinnett, Hodgson, The Countess Wachmeister, The Secret Doctrine, Madame Blavatsky's Protest, Annie Bessant, The Russian Sphinx, The Key to the Cryptogram, The Coming Avatar, The Chosen, The Ancient Wisdom in the Modern World, Where Do the Masters Live and What Do They Do? Etc.

THE ESSENES AND THE KABBALAH Two Essays by Christian D. Ginsburg. Description of the Essenes, Ancient and Modern Literature, The Meaning of the Kabbalah, Kabbalistic Cosmogony, Creation of Angels and Men, The Destiny of Man and the Universe, Kabbalism, the Old Testament, and Christianity, The Books of the Kabbalah, The Schools, Indexes and Glossary.

GEMS OF MYSTICISM by H.A. and F.H. Curtiss. Spiritual Growth, Duty, Karma, Reincarnation, The Christ, Masters of Wisdom.

THE HISTORY AND POWER OF MIND by Richard Ingalese. Divine Mind; It's Nature and Manifestation, Dual Mind and its Origin, Self-Control Re-Embodiment, Colors of Thought Vibration, Meditation, Creation, Concentration, Psychic Forces and their Dangers, Spiritual Forces and Uses, Cause and Cure of Disease, Law Of Opulance.

INFINITE POSSIBILITIES by Leilah Wendell. Essence of Time, Time and Space, Inseperable Brothers, Coexistent Time, Traveling Through Time, Microcosmic Reflections, Cosmic Consciousness, Universe in a Jar, Psychic Alchemy, Divine Element, What Price Immortality?, Practical Infinity, Etc.

VISUALIZATION AND CONCENTRATION AND HOW TO CHOOSE A CAREER by Fenwicke L. Holmes. The Creative Power of Mind, Metaphysics and Psychology, Mental Telepathy, Visualization and Dramatization. Concentration, How to Choose a Career.

GENERAL OCCULT

THE BOOK OF CHARMS AND TALISMANS by Sepharial. History and Background, Numbers and their Significance, Charms to Wear, Background of Talismans, Making Talismans.

BYGONE BELIEFS - AN EXCURSION INTO THE OCCULT AND ALCHEMICAL NATURE OF MAN by H. Stanley Redgrove. Mediaeval Thought, Pythagoras and his Philosophy, Medicine and Magic, Belief in Talismans, Ceremonial Magic in Theory and Practice, Architectural Symbolism, Philosopher's Stone, The Phallic Element in Alchemical Doctrine, Roger Bacon, Etc. (Many Illustrations).

THE COILED SERPENT by C.J. van Vilet. A Philosophy of Conservation and Transmutation of Reproductive Energy. Spirit Versus Matter, Sex Principle and Purpose of Sex, Marriage and Soul-Mates, Love Versus Sex, Erotic Dreams, Perversion and Normalcy, Virility, Health and Disease, Freemasonry, Rosicrucians, Alchemy, Astrology, Theosophy, Magic, Yoga, Occultism, Supermen, Immortality, Etc.

COSMIC SYMBOLISM by Sepharial. Meaning and Purpose of Occultism, Cosmic Symbology, Reading the Symbols, Time Factor in Kabalism, Involution and Evolution, Planetary Numbers, Sounds, Celestial Magnetic Polarities, Law of Vibrations, Lunar and Solar Influences, Astrology and the Law of Sex. Character and Environment, Etc.

THE ELEUSINIAN MYSTERIES AND RITES by Dudley Wright. Eleusinian Legend, Ritual of Mysteries, Program of Greater Mysteries, Intimate Rites, Mystical Significance, Bibliography.

INITIATION AND IT'S RESULTS by Rudolph Steiner. Astral Centers (Chakras), Constitution of the Etheric Body, Dream Life, Three States of Consciousness, Dissociation of Human Personality During Initiation, First Guardian of the Threshold, Second Guardian of the Threshold... Life and Death.

THE INNER GOVERNMENT OF THE WORLD by Annie Besant. Ishvara, The Builders of a Cosmos, The Hierarchy of our World, The Rulers, Teachers, Forces, Method of Evolution, Races and Sub-Races, The Divine Plan, Religions and Civilizations, Etc.

THE MASCULINE CROSS AND ANCIENT SEX WORSHIP by Sha Rocco. Origin of the Cross, Phallus, Marks and Signs of the Triad, Yoni, Color of Gods, Fish and Good Friday, Tortoise, Earth Mother, Fourfold God, Religious Prostitution, Shaga, Communion Buns and Religious Cakes, Antiquity of the Cross, Crucifixion, Christna, Phallic and Sun Worship, Etc.

THE MESSAGE OF AQUARIA by Curtiss. The Mystic Life, The Sign Aquarius, Are These the Last Days?, Comets and Eclipses, Law of Growth, Birth of the New Age, Mastery and the Masters of Wisdom, Mother Earth and the Four Winds, The Spiral of Life and Life Waves, The Message of the Sphinx, Day of Judgement and Law of Sacrifice, The Spiritual Birth, The True Priesthood, Etc.

THE OCCULT ARTS by J.W. Frings. Alchemy, Astrology, Psychometry, Telepathy, Clairvoyance, Spiritualism, Hypnotism, Geomancy, Palmistry, Omens and Oracles.

THE OCCULT ARTS OF ANCIENT EGYPT by Bernard Bromage. Nature of the Ancient Egyptian Civilization, Destiny of Soul, Egyptian Magic and Belief in Amulets and Talismans, Black Magic in Ancient Egypt, The Astrological Implications of Egyptian Magic, Ancient Egypt and Universal Dream Life, Etc. (Includes Various Illustrations).

OCCULTISTS & MYSTICS OF ALL AGES by Ralph Shirley. Apollonius of Tyana, Plotinus, Michael Scot, Paracelsus, Emanuel Swedenborg, Count Cagliostro, Anna Kingsford.

PATIENCE WORTH, A PSYCHIC MYSTERY by Charles S. Yost. The Coming of Patience Worth, Nature of the Communications, Personality of Patience, The Poetry, The Prose, Conversations, Religion, The Ideas on Immortality.

PRACTICAL PSYCHOMANCY AND CRYSTAL GAZING by The "Lyal Series." The Nature of Psychomancy, How to Develope Yourself, Simple Psychomancy, The Astral Tube, Psychometry, Crystal Gazing, Astral Projection, Space, Past Time, Future Time and Dream Psychomancy.

SPIRITISM by Edward B. Warman A.M. Verbal Messages. The Origin of Messages, The Difference Between a Medium and a Psychic, The Physical Phenomena, Independent Slate Writing, etc., Kinetic Energy in Levitation, Materialization, Collective Hallucination, Spirit Photography, Ghosts, Etc.

VOICE OF ISIS by H.A. & F.A. Curtiss. Cycle of Fulfillment, Wisdom Religion, Doctrine of Hell Fire, Eleventh Commandment, Narcotics, Alcohol and Phychism, Karma, Self, Doctrine of Avatara, Reincarnation, Power, A Brief Outline of Evolution, Purity, Origin of Man, Symbol of the Serpent, Purification vs Deification, Memory of Past Lives, Etc.

WHAT IS OCCULTISM? by Papus. Occultism Defined, Philosophical Point of View, Ethics, Aesthetics of Occultism, Theodicy - Sociology, Occultism, The Traditions of Magic, Philosophy.

YOUR UNSEEN GUIDE by C.J. Halsted. Manner in Which You are Guided, How I Am Guided Consciously, Omens, Heaven, Spiritualism, The "Spirit Man," Evidence of My Guide's Prescience, Evolution.

GRAPHOLOGY

HOW TO READ CHARACTER IN HANDWRITING by Mary H. Booth. Principles of Analysis and Deduction, Forming Impressions from Handwriting, Autograph Fad, Entertaining by Graphology, Graphology as a Profession.

HEALING

DIVINE REMEDIES - A TEXTBOOK ON CHRISTIAN HEALING by Theodosia DeWitt Schobert. Healing of Blood Troubles and Skin Diseases, Freedom from Sense Appetite, Healing of Insanity, Insomnia, Poisoning of Any Kind, General Upbuilding and Healing of the Body Temple.

THE FINER FORCES OF NATURE IN DIAGNOSIS AND THERAPY by George Starr White, M.D. Vital and Unseen Forces, Polarity, Cause of Un-Health, Colors, Magnetic Energy, Sympathetic-Vagal Reflex, Human Aura, Moon-Light and Sound Treatment with Light and Color, Etc.

HEAL THYSELF: AN EXPLANATION OF THE REAL CAUSE AND CURE OF DISEASE by Edward Bach, M.B., B.S., D.P.H. by focusing on the causes rather than the results of disease and thus allowing individuals to assist in their own healing, Dr. Bach shows the vital principles which will guide medicine in the near future and are indeed guiding some of the more advanced members of the profession today.

HEALTH AND SPIRITUAL HEALING by Richard Lynch. Key to Health, Rhythm of Life and Health, Realizing the Perfect Body, Tree of Life and Health, How to Renew Your Consciousness, Individual Rebirth in Consciousness, Etc.

THE KEY TO MAGNETIC HEALING by J.H. Strasser. History of Magnetic Healing, Sources of it, Have all Persons Magnetic Power?, Mental Science, Mind and Magnetism, Will Power, Mind over Matter, Why is Suggestion so Effective during Passivity?, To Find Hidden Objects, Hypnotizing at a Distance, Suggestion during Sleep and Waking State, Telepathy, Treatment of Different Diseases, Etc!

THE LOST ART OF HEALING by Agnes J. Galer. What is Truth, The Law of Love, Soul Consciousness, The Heavenly Music, Kingship, Concentration, Illumination, Non-Resistance, The Inner Light, Habits, Health Suggestions and Treatments, Etc.

THE PHILOSOPHY OF MENTAL HEALING - A PRACTICAL EXPOSITION OF NATURAL RESTORATIVE POWER by Leander Edmund Whipple. Metaphysical Healing, Metaphysics Versus Hypnotism, The Potency of Metaphysics in Surgery, Mental Action, The Physical Reflection of Thought, Etc.

THE PRINCIPLES OF OCCULT HEALING Edited by Mary Weeks Burnett, M.D. Occult Healing and Occultism, The Healing Intelligence. The Indestructible Self, Latent Powers of Matter, Auras and Ethers, Polarization, Music, Healing by Prayer, Angel or Deva Helpers, Thought Forms and Color in Healing, Magnetism - Mesmerism, Healing Miracles of Christ, Etc.

SELF HEALING BY THOUGHT FORCE by William Walker Atkinson. The Healing Force, Self Treatment for Equalizing the Circulation, How to Build Up the Organs of Nutrition, Self Treatment for Stomach Troubles and Constipation, Self Treatment for Female Troubles, Self Treatment for Nervousness, Insomnia, Etc.

THE TWELVE HEALERS AND OTHER REMEDIES by Edward Bach. Remedies for the following: Fear, Uncertainty, Insufficient Interest in Present Circumstances, Loneliness, Those Over-Sensitive to Influences and Ideas, Despondency or Despair, Over-Care for Welfare of Others.

HERBS

THE COMPLETE HERBALIST or THE PEOPLE THEIR OWN PHYSICIANS by Dr. O. Phelps Brown. By the use of Nature's Remedies great curative properties found in the Herbal Kingdom are described. A New and Plain System of Hygienic Principles Together with Comprehensive Essays on Sexual Philosophy, Marriage, Divorce, Etc.

THE TRUTH ABOUT HERBS by Mrs. C.F. Loyd. Unbroken Tradition of Herbal Medicine, History of Herbalism, Healing Properties of Certain Herbs, Effect of Herbs on Allergic Diseases, Herbalists' Fight for Freedom, Etc.

HISTORICAL NOVELS

CHILD OF THE SUN: A HISTORICAL NOVEL by Frank Cheavens. Alvar Núñez Cabeza de Vaca was the first European explorer to cross the North American continent. His early 16th century wandering took him across Texas, part of New Mexico, southeastern Arizona, and down the west coast of Mexico. His altruistic work and healing ministrations among the Indians of the Southwest drew to him multitudes who revered him as the Child of the Sun.

HOLLOW EARTH

ETIDORHPA or THE END OF EARTH by John Uri Lloyd. Journey toward center of Earth thru mighty mushroom forests, across huge underground oceans with an entire series of fantastic experiences. A true occult classic! "Etidorhpa, the End of Earth, is in all respects the worthiest presentation of occult teachings under the attractive guise of fiction that has yet been written" - New York World.

INSPIRATION / POSITIVE THINKING / SELF HELP / RECOVERY
(Also see "New Thought")

BEING AND BECOMING - The Principles and Practices of the Science of Spirit by Fenwicke L. Holmes. The Great Law of Mind, Concentration vs. Ideation, Affirmation, Healing Realization, The Purpose of Spirit, The Motive - Love, Love - The Healing Power, Feelings and Emotions, Why Many Fail, Mysticism, Our Power of Choice, Being, Intuition, Spirit as Formative, Demonstrating Prosperity.

CHARACTER - THE GRANDEST THING IN THE WORLD by Orison Swett Marden. A Grand Character, The Light Bearers, The Great-Hearted, Intrepidity of Spirit, "A Fragment of the Rock of Ages," Etc.

CHARACTER BUILDING THOUGHT POWER by Ralph Waldo Trine. "Have we within our power to determine at all times what types of habits shall take form in our lives? In other words, is habit-forming, character-building, a matter of mere chance, or do we have it within our control?"

CREATIVE MIND by Ernest S. Holmes. Why and What is a Man?, Bondage and Freedom, Power We Have Within Us, Reason for the Universe, Mind in Action and Reaction, Arriving at High Consciousness, Perfect Universe, Struggle Karma, Etc.

CRISIS IN CONSCIOUSNESS: The Source of All Conflict by Robert Powell. Importance of Right Beginning, Zen and Liberation, Worldly Mind and Religious Mind, Habit and Freedom, Can Illumination be Transmitted? Must We Have Religious Societies? On Contradiction, Etc.

EVERY LIVING CREATURE or Heart Training Through the Animal World, by Ralph Waldo Trine. "The tender and humane passion in the human heart is too precious a quality to allow it to be hardened or effaced by practices such as we often indulge in." Ralph Waldo Trine.

THE FAITH THAT HEALS (How to develop) by Fenwicke L. Holmes The New Consciousness, Cosmic Consciousness, Practical Use of Visions - Visualizing Prosperity and Health, Cure of Organic Disease and "Incurables," New Healing and Prosperity Consciousness, Your Healing Word, Faith in Yourself, Developing Self-Confidence, etc.

THE FREE MIND: THE INWARD PATH TO LIBERATION by Robert Powell. Liberation and Duality, Living in the Essential, A Noncomparative Look at Zen and Krishnamurti, The Problem of Ambition, Only the Empty Mind is Capable of True Thoughtfulness, If Awareness is Choiceless, Then Who is it That is Aware?, Free Among the Unfree, Etc.

THE GREATEST THING EVER KNOWN by Ralph Waldo Trine. The Greatest Thing Ever Known, Divine Energies in Every-Day Life, The Master's Great but Lost Gift, The Philosopher's Ripest Life Thought, Sustained in Peace and Safety Forever.

HEALTH AND WEALTH FROM WITHIN by William E. Towne. Health From Within, Awakening of Soul, Will, Love and Work, Non-Attachment, Woman - Man, Power of Imagination and Faith, Practical Self-Healing, Etc.

THE HIGHER POWERS OF MIND AND SPIRIT by Ralph Waldo Trine. The Silent, Subtle Building Forces of Mind and Spirit, Thought as a Force in Daily Living, The Divine Rule in the Mind and Heart, The Powerful Aid of the Mind in Rebuilding Body- How Body Helps Mind, Etc.

IN THE FIRE OF THE HEART by Ralph Waldo Trine. With the People: A Revelation, The Conditions that Hold among Us, As Time Deals with Nations, As to Government, A Great People's Movement, Public

Utilities for the Public Good, Labour and Its Uniting Power, Agencies Whereby We Shall Secure the People's Greatest Good, The Great Nation, The Life of the Higher Beauty and Power.

AN IRON WILL by Orison Swett Marden. Training the will, Mental Discipline, Conscious Power, Do You Believe in Yourself? Will Power in its Relation to Health and Disease, The Romance of Achievement Under Difficulties, Concentrated Energy, Staying Power, Persistent Purpose, Success Against Odds, Etc.

THE MAN WHO KNEW by Ralph Waldo Trine. The Power of Love, All is Well, That Superb Teaching of "Sin", He Teaches the Great Truth, When a Brave Man Chooses Death, Bigotry in Fear Condemns and Kills, Love the Law of Life, The Creative Power of Faith and Courage, Etc.

A MESSAGE TO GARCIA and Other Essays by Elbert Hubbard. A Message to Garcia, The Boy from Missouri Valley, Help Yourself by Helping the House. "He was of big service to me in telling me the things I knew, but which I did not know I knew, until he told me." Thomas A. Edison.

THE MIRACLE OF RIGHT THOUGHT by Orison Swett Marden. Working for One Thing and Expecting Something Else, Expect Great Things of Yourself, Self-Encouragement by Self-Suggestion, Change the Thought - Change the Man, The Paralysis of Fear, Getting in Tune, A New Way of Bringing Up Children, Training for Longevity, As A Man Thinketh, Etc.

ON THE OPEN ROAD - Being some thoughts and a Little Creed of Wholesome Living by Ralph Waldo Trine. To realize always clearly, that thoughts are forces, that like creates like and like attracts like, and that to determine one's thinking therefore is to determine one's life.

PATHS TO POWER by Floyd B. Wilson. A psychic Law and Student Work, Power: How to Attain It, Harmony, The Assertion of the I, The Tree of Knowledge, Faith, Wasted Energy, Something About Genius, Etc.

POSITIVE THOUGHTS ATTRACT SUCCESS by Mary A. Dodson and Ella E. Dodson. "Unless We Can Do The Work Better, We Have No Right To Find Fault When Another Does It." "I Am a Holy Temple, and Send Out Love and Good To All The World." "What You Accomplish is Often Determined by What You Attempt." "I will Develop a Powerful Personality." Etc.

SEVEN SECRETS OF SUCCESS by Madison C. Peters, D.D. Do Your Best, Find Out Where Your Talents Lie, Specialize Your Work, Doing Well Depends on Doing Completely, The Blessedness of Being Handicapped, Take Hold of Your Life With a Purpose, The Force of Will, Odd Moments - Success Opportunities, The Failure of Success, Etc.

THE SCIENCE OF GETTING RICH or Financial Success Through Creative Thought by Wallace D. Wattles. The Right to be Rich, There is a Science to Getting Rich, How Riches Come to You, Thinking in a Certain Way, How to Use the Will, Efficient Action, Getting into the Right Business, Etc.

SO SPEAKS HIGHER POWER: A Handbook for Emotional and Spiritual Recovery by Dr. Isaac Shamaya. Addiction, Stress and Recovery, Feeling, Blame, Anger, Fear and Pain, Relationships, Understanding, Love, and Higher Power.

THE SUCCESS PROCESS by Brown Landone. Five Factors Which Guarantee Success. The Process of Vivid Thinking, Tones Used in Persuading, Use of Action, Overcoming Hindrances, Developing Capacities, Securing Justice, Augmenting Your Success by Leadership, Etc.

THIS MYSTICAL LIFE OF OURS A Book of Suggestive Thoughts for Each Week Through the Year by Ralph Waldo Trine. The Creative Power of Thought, The Laws of Attraction, Prosperity, and Habit-Forming, Faith and Prayer - Their Nature, Self-Mastery, Thoughts are Forces, How We Attract Success or Failure, The Secret and Power of Love, Will - The Human and The Divine, The Secret of the Highest Power, Wisdom or Interior Illumination, How Mind Builds Body, Intuition: The Voice of the Soul, To Be at Peace, Etc!

JAMES ALLEN TITLES

ABOVE LIFE'S TURMOIL by James Allen. True Happiness, Immortal Man, Overcoming of Self, Uses of Temptation, Basis of Action, Belief that Saves, Thought and Action, Your Mental Attitude, The Supreme Justice, Use of Reason, Self-Discipline, Resolution, Contentment in Activity, Pleasant Pastures of Peace, Etc.

ALL THESE THINGS ADDED by James Allen. Entering the Kingdom, Soul's Great Need, At Rest in the Kingdom, The Heavenly Life, Divine Center, Eternal Now, "Original Simplicity", The Might of Meekness, Perfect Love, Greatness and Goodness, and Heaven in the Heart, Etc.

AS A MAN THINKETH by James Allen. Thought and Character, Effect of Thought on Circumstances, Effect of Thought on Health and the Body, Thought and Purpose, The Thought-Factor in Achievement, Visions and Ideals, Serenity.

BYWAYS OF BLESSEDNESS by James Allen. Right Beginnings, Small Tasks and Duties, Transcending Difficulties, Hidden Sacrifices, Sympathy, Forgiveness, Seeing No Evil, Abiding Joy, Silentness, Solitude, Understanding the Simple Laws of Life, Happy Endings, Etc.

9

EIGHT PILLARS OF PROSPERITY by James Allen. Discussion on Energy, Economy, Integrity, Systems, Sympathy, Sincerity, Impartiality, Self-reliance, and the Temple of Prosperity

ENTERING THE KINGDOM by James Allen. The Soul's Great Need, The Competitive Laws and the Laws of Love, The Finding of a Principle, At Rest in the Kingdom, And All Things Added.

FROM PASSION TO PEACE by James Allen. Passion, Aspiration, Temptation, Transmutation, Transcendence, Beatitude, Peace.

FROM POVERTY TO POWER by James Allen. The Path to Prosperity, Way Out of Undesirable Conditions, Silent Power of Thought, Controlling and Directing One's Forces, Secret of Health, Success, and Power, The Way of Peace, Power of Meditation, Self and Truth, Spiritual Power, Realization of Selfless Love, Entering into the Infinite, Perfect Peace, Etc.

THE HEAVENLY LIFE by James Allen. The Divine Center, The Eternal Now, "Original Simplicity", Unfailing Wisdom, Might of Meekness, The Righteous Man, Perfect Love, Perfect Freedom, Greatness and Goodness, Heaven in the Heart.

THE LIFE TRIUMPHANT by James Allen. Faith and Courage, Manliness and Sincerity, Energy and Power, Self-Control and Happiness, Simplicity and Freedom, Right-Thinking and Repose, Calmness and Resource, Insight and Nobility, Man and the Master, and Knowledge and Victory.

LIGHT ON LIFE'S DIFFICULTIES by James Allen. The Light that Leads to Perfect Peace, Law of Cause and Effect in Human Life, Values - Spiritual and Material, Adherence to Principle, Management of the Mind, Self-Control, Acts and their Consequences, Way of Wisdom, Individual Liberty, Blessing and Dignity of Work, Diversity of Creeds, War and Peace, Brotherhood of Man, Life's Sorrows, Life's Change, Etc.

MAN: KING OF MIND, BODY AND CIRCUMSTANCE by James Allen. Inner World of Thoughts, Outer World of Things, Habit: Its Slavery and Its Freedom, Bodily Conditions, Poverty, Man's Spiritual Dominion, Conquest: Not Resignation.

THE MASTERY OF DESTINY by James Allen. Deeds, Character and Destiny, Science of Self-Control, Cause and Effect in Human Conduct, Training of the Will, Thoroughness, Mind-Building and Life-Building, Cultivation of Concentration, Practice of Meditation, Power of Purpose, Joy of Accomplishment.

MEDITATIONS, A YEAR BOOK by James Allen. "James Allen may truly be called the Prophet of Meditation. In an age of strife, hurry, religious controversy, heated arguments, ritual and ceremony, he came with his message of Meditation, calling men away from the din and strife of tongues into the peaceful paths of stillness within their own souls, where 'the Light that lighteth every man that cometh into the world' ever burns steadily and surely for all who will turn their weary eyes from the strife without to the quiet within.' Contains two quotes and a brief commentary for each day of the year.

MORNING AND EVENING THOUGHTS by James Allen. Contains a separate and brief paragraph for each morning and evening of the month.

OUT FROM THE HEART by James Allen. Heart and the Life, Nature of Power of Mind, Formation of Habit, Doing and Knowing, First Steps in the Higher Life, Mental Conditions and Their Effects, Exhortation.

THROUGH THE GATE OF GOOD by James Allen. The Gate and the Way, Law and the Prophets, The Yoke and the Burden, The Word and the Doer, The Vine and the Branches, Salvation this Day.

THE WAY OF PEACE by James Allen. The Power of Meditation, The Two Masters: Self and Truth, Spiritual Power, Realization of Selfless Love, Entering into the Infinite, Saints, Sages and Saviors, The Law of Service, Realization of Perfect Peace.

PERSONALITY: ITS CULTIVATION AND POWER AND HOW TO ATTAIN by Lily L. Allen. Personality, Right Belief, Self-Knowledge, Intuition, Decision and Promptness, Self-Trust, Thoroughness, Manners, Physical Culture, Mental, Moral and Spiritual Culture, Introspection, Emancipation, Self-Development, Self-Control and Mental Poise, Liberty, Transformation, Balance, Meditation and Concentration.

KUNDALINI

AND THE SUN IS UP: KUNDALINI RISES IN THE WEST by W. Thomas Wolfe. Hindu's View, Esoteric Christian's View, Professional Specialist's View, The Kundalini Subject's View, Physiological Effects, Spiritual Weightlessness, Emotional and Attitudinal Changes, Changed Dream Content, Reason for Summoning Up Kundalini, Christ and the Kundalini, A Modern Parallel to the Second Coming, Etc.

LIGHT

PHILOSOPHY OF LIGHT - AN INTRODUCTORY TREATISE by Floyd Irving Lorbeer. Light and Perception, Some Cosmic Considerations, Light and Health, Electrical Hypothesis, Temperament, Beauty, and Love, Problem of Space and Time, Unity and Diversity, Deity, Soul and Immortality, Etc.

PRINCIPLES OF LIGHT AND COLOR by Edwin D. Babbitt. (Illustrated, Complete 578p. version.) Harmonic Laws of the Universe, Etherio-Atomic Philosophy of Force, Chromo Chemistry, Chromo

Therapeutics, General Philosophy of Finer Forces. Together with Numerous Discoveries and Practical Applications, Etc!

LONGEVITY

FOREVER YOUNG: HOW TO ATTAIN LONGEVITY by Gladys Iris Clark. Rejuvenation Practices, Youth in Age-Old Wisdom, Longevity Begins with God Awareness, Coping with Realities, Non-Aging Techniques in Action, Etc.

MEDITATION

CONCENTRATION AND MEDITATION by Christmas Humphreys. Importance of Right Motive, Power of Thought, Dangers and Safeguards, Particular Exercises, Time, Place, Posture, Relaxation, Breathing, Thoughts, Counting the Breaths, Visualization and Color, Stillness, Motive, Self Analogy, Higher Meditation, Voice of Mysticism, Jhanas, Zen, Satori, Koan, Ceremonial Magic, Taoism, Occultism, Theosophy, Yoga, The Noble Eightfold Path, Etc.

METAPHYSICAL NOVELS

THE HOUSE OF FULFILLMENT, The Romance of the Soul by L. Adams Beck. "The supernormal happenings in this romance are true to and are founded upon the Ancient Indian Philosophy of the Upanishads." L. Adams Beck.

MYRIAM AND THE MYSTIC BROTHERHOOD by Maude Lesseuer Howard. A novel in the western mystic tradition.

THE PEOPLE OF THE MIST by H. Rider Haggard. Author of *Allan Quartermain, She, King Solomon's Mines, Etc.* "*The People of the Mist* belongs to the sphere of *She* in it's imaginative scope, and, as an example of the storyteller's art, must be reckoned of the excellent company of *King Solomon's Mines* and its bretheren." *Saturday Review.*

WITHIN THE TEMPLE OF ISIS by Belle M. Wagner. The Revelation of the Astrologer, In the Presence of the Heirophant, The Midnight of the Full Moon, Within the Adytum, The Transfer, The Awakening, A Visit to the Chief Astrologer, Princess Nu-Nah, The Initiation, The Princess' Wedding, The Retirement, The Return to New Life.

MUSIC

MUSIC: ITS SECRET INFLUENCE THROUGHT THE AGES by Cyril Scott. The Effects of Sound and Music, Musicians and the Higher Power, The Occult Constitution of Man, The Beginnings of Music and Religion, Effects of Music on the Indian People, Ancient Egyptians, Greeks and Romans, The Music of the Future, Etc.

MYTHOLOGY

A DICTIONARY OF NON-CLASSICAL MYTHOLOGY by Marian Edwardes & Lewis Spence. An exceptional work! "Not one mythology, but several, will be found concentrated within the pages of this volume..." Covers everything from Aah (Ah): An Egyptian moon-god, thru Brigit: A goddess of the Irish Celts, Excalibur: King Arthur's Sword, Hou Chi: A Chinese divine personage, ... Huitzilopochtli of the Aztecs ... Mama Cocha of Peru ... Uttu: The Sumerian ... Valkyrie (Old German): Female warriors ... Byelun: A white Russian deity, ... Meke Meke: The god-creator of Easter Island, Mwari: The Great Spirit of the Mtawara tribe of Rhodesia, Triglav (Three heads): Baltic Slav deity... and hundreds more!

NEW THOUGHT (Also see "Inspiration")

THE GIFT OF THE SPIRIT A Selection From the Essays of Prentice Mulford Infinite Mind in Nature, God in Yourself, Doctor Within & Mental Medicine, Faith or Being Led by the Spirit, Material Mind vs. Spiritual Mind, What are Spintual Gifts?, Regeneration or Being Born Again, Re-Embodiment Universal in Nature, You Travel When You Sleep, Prayer In All Ages, Etc.

THE GIFT OF UNDERSTANDING by Prentice Mulford. Force and How to Get It, The Source of Your Strength, The Drawing Power of Mind, The Necessity of Riches, Love Thyself, How Thoughts are Born, The Art of Forgetting, Etc.

HEALTH AND POWER THROUGH CREATION by Paul Ellsworth. The Secret of Mastery, The Divine Mind, How to Awaken Sleeping Power, Building a Master Memory, The Secret of Dynamic Thinking, Physical Immortality, How to Build Success, The Three Planes of Healing, Etc.

THE HEART OF THE NEW THOUGHT by Ella Wheeler Wilcox. Let the Past Go, Thought Force, Opulence and Eternity, Morning Influences, Philosophy of Happiness, Common Sense, The Object of Life, Wisdom and Self Conquest, Concentration and Destiny, The Breath, Generosity and Balance, Etc.

THE HIDDEN POWER AND OTHER PAPERS UPON MENTAL SCIENCE by Thomas Troward. Hidden Power, Perversion of Truth, The "I Am", Affirmative Power, Principle of Guidance, Desire as Motive Power, Spirit of Opulence, Beauty, Separation and Unity, Entering into Spirit, Bible and New Thought, What is Higher Thought?, Etc!

HOW TO USE NEW THOUGHT IN HOME LIFE by Elizabeth Towne. How Concentration Eliminates

Drudgery, On Pulling Together, How to Live With a Groucher, Making Love a Habit of Thought, Express Yourself, Etc.

THE LAW OF THE NEW THOUGHT by Willam Walker Atkinson. What is New Thought?, Thoughts are Things, Law of Attraction, Mind Building, Subconsious Plane, Oneness of All, Immortality of the Soul, Unfoldment, Growth of Consciouness, Soul's Awakening.

MIND REMAKES YOUR WORLD Edited by Ernest Holmes and Maude Allison Lathem. The Creative Principle at Work, The New Teaching for the New Age, Divine Science, The Awakening Power of Christ, Ontology, The Science of Being, Practical Recipes, Etc.

NEW THOUGHT ESSAYS by Charles Brodie Patterson. Life as a Journey, The Mental Origin of Disease, How We Make Our Environment, The Evolution of Power, Breath Vibration, Mental Science vs Hypnotism, Thoughts on Spiritual Healing, Healing at a Distance, Etc.

NEW THOUGHT HEALING MADE PLAIN by Kate Atkinson Boehme. Thought is a Force, The Subconscious Mind, The Superconscious Mind, How to Heal Yourself and Others, Ensouling Thought Forms, Tapping Higher Levels of Energy, Affirmations for Achievement, Etc.

PROSPERITY THROUGH THOUGHT FORCE by Bruce MacLelland. Concerning Elements, The Law of Imagination, The Mental Attitude, Better Sometimes to Forget, Physical Effort vs Mental Attraction, Fear of Failure Brings it to You, Etc.

THOUGHT FORCES by Prentice Mulford. Practical Mental Recipes, Drawing Power of Mind, Buried Talents, Necessity of Riches, Uses of Sickness, The Doctor Within, Mental Medicine, Use and Necessity of Recreation, Art of Forgetting, Cultivate Repose, Love Thyself. Etc.

THOUGHTS ARE THINGS by Prentice Mulford. Material Mind vs Spiritual Mind, Who Are Our Relations?, Thought Currents, One Way to Cultivate Courage, God in the Trees, Some Laws of Health and Beauty, The God in Yourself, Healing and Renewing Force of Spring, Attraction of Aspiration, Etc.

TRAINING OF CHILDREN IN THE NEW THOUGHT by Frances Partlow. First Steps, Growing, Strengthening the Bonds, Bending Twigs, Asserting the Self, The Universal Mother, Death and After, The Magnetism of Character, "You Can" and "You Will," Entering the Silence, Etc.

THE WILL TO BE WELL by Charles Brodie Patterson. The Unity of Life, The Law of Attraction, Mental Influences, The Laws of Health, Spiritual Treatment, The Life of Power, The Way of Salvation, The Spirit of Praise, The Dawn of a New Age, Health of Mind and Body. Etc.

YOUR FORCES AND HOW TO USE THEM by Prentice Mulford. Woman's Real Power, Love Thyself, Mental Medicine, Prayer in all Ages, Good and Ill Effects of Thought, Buried Talents, Etc.

NUMEROLOGY

NAMES, DATES, AND NUMBERS - A SYSTEM OF NUMEROLOGY by Roy Page Walton. Law of Numbers, Character and influence of Numbers, Application and Use of Numbers, Strong and Weak Names, The Number that Governs Life, How Each Single Name Effects Life, The Importance of Varying the Signature, How the Name Discloses the Future, Choosing a Suitable Name for a Child, Names Suitable for Marriage, How to Find Lucky Days and Months. Points to Bear in Mind.

NUMBERS: THEIR OCCULT POWER AND MYSTIC VIRTUE by W. Wynn Wescott. Pythagoras, His Tenets and His Followers, Pythagorean Views of Numbers, Kabalistic View on Numbers, Properties of the Numbers According to the Bible, the Talmuds, the Pythagoreans, the Romans, Chaldeans, Egyptians, Hindoos, Medieval Magicians, Hermetic Students, and the Rosicurcians.

NUMBER VIBRATION IN QUESTIONS AND ANSWERS by Mrs. L. Dow Balliett. When Was Your First Birth?, First Step in Reading a Name, Can Name be Changed?, What Does Birth Path Show?, Numerical and Number Chart, Is Esoteric Value to be Found in Gems?, Why Do We Not Add Either 22 or 11?, Day of Reincarnation, Is Anybody Out of Place?, Are We Gods?, Of What Use is Prayer?, What Is the Soul?, Should Rooms be Furnished in our Own Colors?, What Months Are Best for Creation?, What Is Astral Music?, Where Should We Live?. Etc. Etc. Etc!

NUMERAL PHILOSOPHY by Albert Christy. A Study of Numeral Influences upon the Physical, Mental, and Spiritual Nature of Mankind.

VIBRATION: A SYSTEM OF NUMBERS AS TAUGHT BY PYTHARGORAS by Mrs. L. Dow Balliett. The Principles of Vibration, Numbers in Detail, What Your Name Means (broadly speaking), Business, Choosing a Husband or Wife, Pythagoras' Laws, Your Colors, Body Parts, Gems, Minerals, Flowers, Birds, Odors, Music, Guardian Angel, Symbols, Etc.

ORIENTAL (Also see "YOGA")

BUDDHA, TRUTH, AND BROTHERHOOD an Epitome of Many Buddhist Scriptures Translated from the Japanese, Edited by Dwight Goddard. The Teaching of the Buddha, His Compassion and Vows, Buddha's Three Bodies, The Four Noble Truths, The Middle Way, The Human Mind and the True Mind, Worldly Passions, Purification of Mind, Teaching of Ancient Fables, The Way Of Concentration, Practical Guide to True Living, Etc.

12

THE BUDDHA'S GOLDEN PATH by Dwight Goddard. Prince Siddhartha Gautama, Right Ideas, Speech, Right Vocation, Words, Conduct, Mindfulness, Concentration, Resolution, Environment, Intuition, Vows, Spiritual Behaviour, Spirit, Etc.

A BUDDHIST CATECHISM an Outline of the Doctrine of the Buddha Gotama by Subhádra Bhikshu. The Buddha, The Doctrine (Dhamma), The Brotherhood of the Elect (Sangha), Vesres from the Dhammapada.

BUSHIDO: WAY OF THE SAMURAI Translated from the classic Hagakure by Minoru Tanaka. This unique translation of a most important Japanese classic offers an explanation of the central and upright character of the Japanese people, and their indomitable inner strength.

DAO DE JING (LAO-ZI): THE OLD SAGE'S CLASSIC OF THE WAY OF VIRTUE translated by Patrick Michael Byrne. A new translation, faithful to both the letter and the poetic spirit of the original, of the ancient Chinese book of wisdom (traditionally known as the *Tao Te Ching* of Lao Tse or Lao Tsu: this version employs the new, more accurate *pinyin* transliteration). With introduction, notes and commentary.

THE DHARMA or the Religion of Enlightenment; an Exposition of Buddhism by Dr. Paul Carus. Twelve Articles Characteristic of Buddhism, The Four Noble Truths, Avoiding the Ten Evils, Law of Causation, The Abhidharma Outlined, Karma, Atman, The Soul, Reincarnation, The Eternal Man, Nirvana, The Buddhist Faith, A Summary of the Tenets of Buddhism, Etc.

FUSANG or THE DISCOVERY OF AMERICA BY CHINESE BUDDHIST PRIESTS IN THE FIFTH CENTURY by Charles G. Leland. Chinese Knowledge of Lands and Nations, The Road to America, The Kingdom of Fusang or Mexico, Laws and Customs of the Aztecs, The Future of Eastern Asia, Travels of Other Buddhist Priests, Affinities of American and Asiatic Languages, Images of Buddha, Etc.

HINDU PHILOSOPHY IN BRIEF by Edward B. Warman A.M. What is this Philosophy? The Hindu Triad, The Bhagavad Gita, Buddha, Om, Vedas, Krishna, Guru, The Garden of Eden, The Trees of Knowledge and Life, Huras, Astral Bodies, Karma, Reincarnation, Yoga, The Vedanta Philosophy, The Deluge, Asanas and Pranayama, Etc.

THE HISTORY OF BUDDHIST THOUGHT by Edward J. Thomas. The Ascetic Ideal, Early Doctrine: Yoga, Brahminism and the Upanishads, Karma, Release and Nirvana, Buddha, Popular Bodhisattva Doctrine, Buddhism and Modern Thought, Etc.

THE IMITATION OF BUDDHA - Quotations from Buddist Literature for Each Day of the Year Compiled by Ernest M. Bowden with preface by Sir Edwin Arnold. These 366 wonderful quotes are taken from a broad base of Buddhist Literature including many now hard-to-find texts.

THE MYSTERY OF BEING or Oriental Teachings vs Occidental Theories by Heeralal Dhole. Sankhya System, Properties of Matter, Gunas, Mind, Primordal Element, Matter and Force, Human Aggregate, Origin of Life, Doctrine of Causality, Pantheism vs Anthropomorphism.

THE NEW AGE I CHING by Gordan. This book offers a revolutionary approach seeking to understand the oracle from the perspective of our modern age, neither repeating old ideas by rote nor rejecting them for their archaic style, but attempting to relearn their wisdom again.

RAMA TIRTHA, SCIENTIST AND MAHATMA by Hari Prasad Shastri. A Short Account of the Life of Rama Tirtha, The Object and Need of Worship, Impediments to Concentration, The Need of Generosity and Devotion, Is Soliciting Part of Worship? Worship and Knowledge, Perfect Purity, The Mantras for Worship, The Benefit of Meditation, The Jnani, Etc.

SACRED BOOKS OF THE EAST by Epiphanius Wilson. Vedic Hymns, The Zend-Avesta, The Dhammapada, The Upanishads, Selections from the Koran, Life of Buddha, Etc.

THE TEXT OF YI KING and its appendixes, Chinese Original With English Translation by Z. D. Sung. The Text, The Appendixes, The Great Appendix, Treatise of Remarks in the Trigrams, The Orderly Sequence of the Trigrams, Treatise on the Hexagrams Taken Promiscuously.

THE WISDOM OF THE HINDUS by Brian Brown. Brahmanic Wisdom, Maha-Bharata, The Ramayana, Wisdom of the Upanishads, Vivekananda and Ramakrishna on Yoga Philosophy, Wisdom of Tuka-Ram, Paramananda, Vivekananda, Abbedananda, Etc.

PALMISTRY

INDIAN PALMISTRY by Mrs. J. B. Dale. Signification of Animals, Flowers, and Promiscuous Marks, The Mounts, Line of Life, The Line of the Head and Brain, Line of Fortune, Venus and Mars, Rule to Tell the Planets, Mount of Jupiter, Apollo the Sun, The Moon, Mount of Saturn, Planet Mercury, Mensa: The Part of Fortune, Fingers and Thumb, Head and Signs of the Feet and Arms, Etc.

PHILOSOPHY

GOETHE - WITH SPECIAL CONSIDERATION OF HIS PHILOSOPHY by Paul Carus. The Life of Goethe, His Relation to Women, Goethe's Personality, The Religion of Goethe, Goethe's Philosophy, Literature and Criticism, The Significance of "Faust", Miscellaneous Epigrams and Poems. (Heavily Illustrated).

PROPHECY (Also See "Earth Changes")

THE STORY OF PROPHECY by Henry James Forman. What is Prophecy?, Oracles, The Great Pyramid Speaks, The End of the Age: Biblical Prophecy, Medieval Prophecy, Astrologers and Saints, Prophecies Concerning the Popes, Nostradamus, America In Prophecy, The Prophetic Future.

THE BOOK OF REVELATION by Clarence Larkin. The Things Which Though Hast Seen, The Things Which Are, The Things Which Shall be Hereafter, The Seven Seals, Trumpets, Personages, Vials, Dooms, New Things. Includes Numerous Illustrations, Charts, Maps, and Cuts.

PYRAMIDOLOGY

THE GREAT PYRAMID. Two Essays plus illustrations, one from The Reminder and the other from J.F. Rowney Press. Selections include: The Pyramid's Location and Constructional Features, Some of the Pyramid's Scientific Features, Complete History of Mankind Represented in the Pyramid, The Symbolism of the Passages and Chambers, Etc.

THE GREAT PYRAMID - Its Construction, Symbolism, and Chronology by Basil Stewart. Construction and Astrological Features, Chart of World History, Missing Apex-stone, Who Built It? Plus Various Diagrams.

REINCARNATION

LIFE AFTER LIFE: THE THEORY OF REINCARNATION by Eustace Miles. Have We Lived Before? Questions Often Asked, Does Not Oppose Christianity, Great Men Who Have Believed, Etc.

THE NEW REVELATION by Sir Arthur Conan Doyle. The Search, The Revelation, The Coming Life, Problems and Limitations, The Next Phase of Life, Automatic Writing, The Cheriton Dugout.

REINCARNATION by George B. Brownell. Memories of Past Lives, A Remarkable Proof, Lived Many Lives, An Arabian Incarnation, Dreamed of Past Life, Great Minds and Reincarnation, The Bible and Reincarnation, Karma, Atlantis Reborn, Thought is Destiny, The Celestial Body, The Hereafter, Etc.

REINCARNATION by F. Homer Curtiss, M.D. The Doctrine, Why and How, In the New Testament, Objections Answered, Scientific Evidence and Physical Proof.

REINCARNATION by Katherine Tingley. What Reincarnation Is, Arguments for Reincarnation, Supposed Objections to Reincarnation, Reincarnation and Heredity, Reincarnation in Antiquity, Reincarnation the Master-Key to Modern Problems, Reincarnation In Modern Literature.

THE RING OF RETURN by Eva Martin. Pre-Christian Era, Early Christian and Other Writings of the First Five Centuries A.D., Miscellaneous Sources Before A.D. 1700, A.D. 1700-1900, The Twentieth Century. In this book, Miss Eva Martin has brought together a most complete and scholarly collection of references to past, present, and future life.

RELIGIONS

THE BIBLE IN INDIA - Hindoo Origin of Hebrew and Christian Revelation Translated from "La Bible Dans L'Inde" by Louis Jacolliot. India's Relation to Antiquity, Zeus - Jezeus - Isis - Jesus, Moses Founds Hebrew Society on the Model of Egypt and India, The Hindoo Genesis, The Hindoo Trinity, Adima (In Sanscrit, The First Man), The Deluge According to the Maha-Barata, Prophecies Announcing the Coming of Christna, Massacre of all Male Children Born on the Same Night as Christna, Parable of the Fisherman, Christna's Philosophic Teaching, Transfiguration of Christna, His Disiples Give Him The Name of Jezeus (Pure Essence), Christna and the Two Holy Women, Death of Christna, Hindoo Origin of the Christian Idea, Christna and Christ, Etc!

CREATIVE PRAYER by E. Herman. Prayer as Creative Energy, The Ministry of Silence, The Discipline of Meditation, From Self to God, The Path to Power, The Apostolate of Power, The Priesthood of Prayer.

THE MYSTICAL QUEST OF CHRIST by Robert F. Horton M.A., D.D. The Rule of Life, The Choice of a Calling, The Christian Decalogue, Extending the Kingdom of Heaven, All Nations Near to God, Forgiveness of Injuries, "Go Thou and Do Likewise," The Esteem of the Poor, Honesty, Health. Peace, The Sacredness of Child Life, Autosuggestion, Mysticism, The Evangelic Virtues, Etc.

NATURAL LAW IN THE SPIRITUAL WORLD by Henry Drummond. Biogenesis, Degeneration, Growth, Death, Mortification, Eternal Life, Environment, Conformity to Type, Semi-Parasitism, Parasitism, Classification.

THE PLEROMA an Essay on the Origin of Christianity by Dr. Paul Carus. Christianity Determined by the Needs of the Age, The Old Paganism, Pre-Christian Gnostiticism, The Gnostic Movement, Kindred Sects, How the Gentile Saviour Changed into the Christ, The Origin of Judaism, The Judaism of Jesus, The Future of Christianity, Etc.

PRINCIPAL SYMBOLS OF WORLD RELIGIONS by Swami Harshananda. Chapters include discussions of the symbols of these religions: Hinduism, Buddhism, Jainism, Sikhism, Shintoism, Islam, Christianity, Judaism, Zoroastrianism, Taoism.

THE RELIGION OF THE SIKH GURUS by Teja Singh, M.A., Teja Singh, formerly a professor of history at Khalsa College in Amritsar, outlines the foundation of history, tradition, ritual and principles which

14

has kept disciples of the the Sikh religion strong and united into the present day.

WIT AND WISDOM OF THE TALMUD Edited by Madison C. Peters, D.D. Actions, Ambition, Anger, Associates, Charity, Contentment, Cruelity to Animals, Death, Fools, Friendship, Guilt, Home Life, Honesty, Huminity, Immortality, Judging, Justice, Labor, The Law, Love, Mercy, Money, Obedience, Passion, Patriotism, Peacefulness, Persecution, Physications, Prayer, Public Opinion, Religion, Repentance, Resignation, Revenge, The Righteous, Robbery, Secrets, Self-Respect, Sin, Slander, The Soul, Tolerance, Truth, Usuary, Wisdom, Woman, Youth, Etc!

SELF-HELP / RECOVERY (See under "Inspiration, etc.")

SOUL

THE HUMAN SOUL IN SLEEPING, DREAMING AND WAKING by F.W. Zeylmans van Emmichoven, M.D. What is the Soul?, Dreams, The Awakening of the Soul, Fears, Meditation, Concentration and Self Development, Etc.

THE INNER MAN by Hanna Hurnard. A Parable, The Inner Man, Communication with the Heavenly World, The Soul of the Inner Man, The Garments of the Soul, Soul Disease and Soul Healing, The Soul's Psychic Powers, The Mystic Way.

TAROT

THE ILLUSTRATED KEY TO THE TAROT - THE VEIL OF DIVINATION by Arthur Edward Waite. The Veil and Its Symbols, The Tarot in History, The Doctrine Behind the Veil, The Outer Method of the Oracles, The Four Suits of Tarot Cards, The Art of Tarot Divination. An Ancient Celtic Method of Divination.

THE KEY OF DESTINY by H.A. and F.H. Curtiss. The Initiate, Twelve-fold Division of the Zodiac, Reincarnation and Transmutation, The Solar System, The Letters of the Tarot, The Numbers 11 thru 22, Twelve Tribes and Twelve Disciples, The Great Work, The Labors of Hercules, Necromancy, Great Deep, Temperance, Man the Creator vs the Devil, Celestial Hierarchies, The New Jerusalem, Etc.

THE KEY TO THE UNIVERSE by H.A. and F.H. Curtiss. Origin of the Numerical Systems, Symbol of the "0" and the Serpent, The "0" as the Egg and the Cat, The "0" as the Aura and the Ring Pass Not, Symbol of the "0", Letters of the Tarot, The Numbers 1 thru 10, The 7 Principles of Man, The 7 Pleiades and the 7 Rishis, Joy of Completion.

WESTERN MYSTICISM

ANCIENT MYSTERY AND MODERN REVELATION by W.J. Colville. Faiths of Man in All Lands, Ancient and Modern Ideas of Revelation - Its Sources and Agencies, Creation Legends - How Ancient is Humanity On this Planet? Egypt and Its Wonders, Philosophy of Ancient Greece, School of Pythagoras, Delphic Mysteries, Apollonius of Tyana, Five Varieties of Yoga, Union of Eastern and Western Philosophy, Ezekiel's Wheel - What it Signifies, Book of Exodus - Its Practical and Esoteric Teachings, Message of Buddhism - Purity and Philanthropy, Magic in Europe in the Middle Ages, Ancient Magic and Modern Therapeutics, Bible Symbolism, Teachings of the Gnostics.

BROTHERHOOD OF MT. SHASTA by Eugene E. Thomas. From Clouds to Sunshine, Finding the Brotherhood, The Lake of Gold, The Initiation, Memories of the Past, In Advance of the Future, Prodigy, Trial and Visitor, The Annihilation and the King, The Lost Lemuria.

THE CANDLE OF VISION by A.E. Meditation, The Memory of Earth, Imagination, The Architecture of Dreams, Intuition, The Language of the Gods, Ancient Intuitions, Power, The Memory of Spirit, Celtic Cosmology, The Celtic Imigination, Earth, Etc.

CLOTHED WITH THE SUN - Being the Book of the Illuminations of Anna (Bonus) Kingsford Edited by Edward Maitland and Samuel Hopgood Hart. Concerning the three Veils between Man and God, Powers of the Air, Devil and Devils, Gods, Psyche or Superior Human Soul, Dying, Mysteries of God, Divine Image or Vision of Adonai, Etc.

COSMOLOGY, RELIGION AND PHILOSOPHY by Rudolph Steiner. The Three Steps of Anthroposophy, Exercises of Thought, Feeling and Volition, Experiences of the Soul in Sleep, The Relation of Christ with Humanity, The Event of Death and its Relationship with the Christ, On Experiencing the Will-Part of the Soul, Etc.

THE GOLDEN VERSES OF PYTHAGORAS AND OTHER PYTHAGOREAN FRAGMENTS Selected and Arrainged by Florence Firth, Introduction by Annie Bessant. The Golden Verses of Pythagoras, Notes on the Verses from the Commentaries of Hierocles, The Sentences of Democrates, Demophilus, Stobaeus, Sextus the Pythagorean and Lamblichus, The Symbols of Pythagoras, Etc.

THE PERFECT WAY or THE FINDING OF CHRIST by Anna (Bonus) Kingsford M.D. and Edward Maitland. The Soul and the Substance of Existance, The Atonement, The Nature and Constitution of the Ego, The Fall, The Redemption, God as the Lord and the Divine Image in the Bible, Kabbala, Bhagavat Gita, The Vision of Adonai, Etc.

INNER RADIANCE by H.A. & F.A. Curtiss. The Inner Radiance, Spiritual Co-operation, Man and the Zodiac, The Soul-Language, Transmigration, Cosmic Cause of World Conditions, Planetary and Karmic Factors, The Mystic Rose, The Lords of Karma, The Great Works, The Mystery of the Elements, The Third

Eye, The Round Table, The Ancient Continents, Nature's Symbology.

KALEVALA: THE LAND OF THE HEROES Translated by W. F. Kirby. The National Epic of Finland. "...the Kalevala itself could one day become as important for all of humanity as Homer was for the Greeks."

THE LOTUS PATH by Elizabeth Delvine King. Illumination, The One Essence Divine, The Fourth Dimension, Vibrations, The Heart Center, Finding Atman, At-One-Ment with the Great "I Am," Freedom, The Balance, Is Prayer Essential? Light - The Source, The Infinite, Ocean Divine, The Oneness, Etc.

THE MASONIC INITIATION by W.L. Wilmshurst. Masonry and Tradition, From Darkness to Light, Initiation - Real and Ceremonial, The Purpose of the Mysteries, Light on the Way, The Knowledge of Yourself, The Superstructure, Seeking a Master, The Grand Lodge Above, Fulness of Light, Apocalypsis, The Past and Future of the Masonic Order, Etc!

THE FOUR GREAT INITIATIONS, by Ellen Conroy M.A.. Foreward by Leon Dabo, Initiation by Water, Mystical Understanding of Baptism, Temptation, Power of the Spirit, Initiation by Air, Mystical Understanding of the Plucking of Corn on the Sabbath Day, Sermon on the Mount, Initiation by Fire, Transfiguration, Initiation by Earth, Crucifiction and Ascension.

THE WAY OF ATTAINMENT by Sydney T. Klein. The Invisible is the Real, The Power of Prayer, Spiritual Regeneration, Dogma of the Virgin Birth, Finding the Kingdom of Heaven "Within", Realizing Oneness with God, Nature of the Ascent, Reaching the Summit.

THE WAY OF MYSTICISM by Joseph James. God Turns Towards Man, The Unexpected, The Still Small Voice, His Exceeding Brightness, Man Turns Towards God, The Obstructive "Me", Where East and West Unite, Beside the Still Waters, Love's Meeting Place, Work - A Prayer, Every Pilgrim's Progress, Love's Fulfillment.

YOGA (also see ORIENTAL)

THE POPULAR PRACTICE OF YOGA by K. V. Mulbagala. Mind and its Functions, Eight Subdivisions of Preliminary Yoga, Significance of OM and the Soul, God, Primordial Matter and Creation, The Innate Powers of the Soul, Success, Breath, Yoga Postures, Final Emancipation, Etc.

YOGA PHILOSOPHY AND PRACTICE by Hari Prasad Shastri. History and Literature of Yoga, Epics and Bhagavad Gita, Patanjali, Philosophy of Yoga, Vedanta, Reason and Intuition, The Teacher (Guru), God and the World, The Nature of the Self, Ethics, Action (Karma), Death and Reincarnation, Liberation, The Practice of Yoga, Peace of Mind, True Self, Dream and Sleep, Vital Currents of the Body, OM, Posture, Pranayama (Control of the Vital Currents), Concentration, Liberation in Life, Common Sense Training, Illustrative Passages from the Literature of Yoga. Upanishads, Bhagavad Gita, Glossary, Etc.

THE SUN (1974 COMPLETE SET OF 4 ISSUES)

TABLOID METAPHYSICAL MAGAZINE The Astral Projection. Metaphysical Tabloid Magazine from the early 1970's. Last three issues available.

GENERAL NON-METAPHYSICAL

BEST ENGRAVINGS Edited by Skip Whitson. One hundred twenty three beautiful steel cut and wood cut engravings from the nineteenth century.

BUSTED IN MEXICO by Ann Palmer and Jessica Herman. One young woman's story of the devastating effects of the loss of liberty. A True Story, Introduction by Governor Jerry Apodaca.

THE LAND OF ENCHANTMENT FROM PIKE'S PEAK TO THE PACIFIC by Lilian Whiting. With Western Stars and Sunsets, Denver the Beautiful, The Picturesque Region of Pike's Peak, Summer Wanderings in Colorado, The Colorado Pioneers, The Surprises of New Mexico, The Story of Santa Fe, Magic and Mystery of Arizona, The Petrified Forest and the Meteorite Mountain, Los Angeles, The Spell-Binder, Grand Canyon, the Carnival of the Gods.

SUN HISTORICAL SERIES Dozens of titles ranging from Maine 100 years ago to Hawaii 100 years ago.

MAYDAYS AND MERMAIDS by William A. Davis. A contemporary tale of the sea. Vivid fast moving satirical yarn, spun on the paradoxical spool of tragicomedy. "Once you start this book there is a high probability that you will not put it down." - Clark Chambers, Critic.

For a PRICE LIST of all currently available Sun Books titles write: Book List, Sun Publishing Co., P.O. Box 5588, Santa Fe, NM 87502-5588